Focu your Family for Under a Fiver

This is a **FLAME TREE** book
First published in 2010

Author: Simoney Girard
Publisher and Creative Director: Nick Wells
Project Editor: Catherine Taylor
Art Director: Mike Spender
Layout Design: Dave Jones
Digital Design and Production: Chris Herbert
Picture Research: Catherine Taylor and Toria Lyle

Special thanks to Gina Steer, Kayla Yurick

10 12 14 13 11
1 3 5 7 9 10 8 6 4 2

This edition first published 2010 by
FLAME TREE PUBLISHING
Crabtree Hall, Crabtree Lane
Fulham, London SW6 6TY
United Kingdom

www.flametreepublishing.com

Flame Tree is part of The Foundry Creative Media Co. Ltd
© The Foundry Creative Media Co. Ltd

ISBN 978-1-84786-703-2

A CIP Record for this book is available from the British Library upon request

Printed in China

Simoney Girard's acknowledgements:
Many thanks to my mum, Veronica Girard, for teaching me to cook when I was seven years old.
The various sources used when compiling the information in this book include: US Department of Agriculture;
Center for Nutrition Policy and Promotion; UK National Health Service (NHS); UK Office for National Statistics;
World Health Organization; *The Metro Recipe Book*, South Metropolitan Gas Company, 1936, courtesy of Beryl
Girard; *Apple Pie and the Maple Leaf: 100 Years of Canadian Home Cooking*, unpublished, author's family's own;
Victory Cookbook: Nostalgic Food and Facts from 1940–1954, Maguerite Patten OBE in association with the
Imperial War Museum, courtesy of Barbara Brine; www.storingandfreezing.co.uk; www.fruitexpert.co.uk; and
www.lovefoodhatewaste.com.

The case studies are based on real families known to the author (names may have been changed to protect identities).

All pictures courtesy of Foundry Arts except the following, which are courtesy of Shutterstock and © the following photographers:
1 Andrew Horwitz; 3 Tiggy Gallery!; 4 & 11 & 12 Losevsky Pavel; 5b & 100 Robyn Mackenzie; 5c & 78 shuqiong; 5t &
54 Nikola Bilic; 6b & 166 Philip Hunton; 6c & 148, 16, 21, 48, 53 Monkey Business Images; 6t & 128, 46 Joe Gough;
7b & 236 David P. Smith; 7t & 198 jokerpro; 8 BlueOrange Studio; 9 niderlander; 10 Leah-Anne Thompson; 14
Provasilich; 19 Brian A Jackson; 22 Chepko Danil Vitalevich; 25 Elena Elisseeva; 27 Stanislav Crnjak; 28 hardtmuth; 29
cen; 31 V. J. Matthew; 32 Carlos Caetano; 35 amfoto; 36 Akhilesh; 37 Silvia Bogdanski; 38 sban; 39 Picsfive; 41
Zhiltsov Alexandr; 42 M.antonis; 45 dimitris_k; 50 hfng

Recipe Editor: Gina Steer

Series Foreword: Tony Turnbull

Feed your Family for Under a Fiver

Simple, Everyday solutions, Recipes, Hints and Tips

FLAME TREE
PUBLISHING

Contents

Setting a budget and sticking to the list can be difficult, but it is important to think about the food you actually need, rather than buying on impulse. This chapter shows how organisational skills and willpower are crucial to saving money on your food shop. Where can you find the best discounts – and when? Perhaps you can cut the family's food budget by shopping elsewhere, or at a different time of the day. You will also learn how to continue saving money once you're cooking – from best practices to how to stretch meals further and how to store leftovers to avoid waste and get more for your money. In 'Challenge: Meals for Under a Fiver', learn about how to exploit the versatility of ingredients and use cheaper cuts of meat, and read a case study. Finally, read the list of store-cupboard ingredients that are suggested as the basis of your cooking arsenal and necessary in many of the recipes to follow – these are items you will only need to buy infrequently.

Recipes: Soups & Starters 54

A great-value dish to prepare, soup can be very cheap to make and still be filling, tasty and nutritious. This section boasts some tempting recipes, from a chunky Italian Bean Soup to a delicious Cream of Pumpkin Soup. There are also some great ideas for starters – why not have fun with Sweetcorn Fritters or try Pasta with Walnut Sauce as a starter or light main meal? All these recipes have been carefully selected for their budget-friendly nature and should easily come in under £5.

Fish & Seafood 78

Fish need not be expensive, as you will have learned in the first section of this book. There are some mouthwatering and hearty dishes suggested here, from Smoked Haddock Kedgeree to Fish Crumble. For seafood options, try the delightful Mussels Linguine or the lip-smacking Pea & Prawn Risotto.

Pork 100

Pork comes in many tasty forms available to those on a tight budget. This section reveals a choice selection of tasty dishes that can be made with bacon, ham, sausages, mince and cheaper cuts of pork. Try the exciting Spanish-style Pork Stew or the satisfying Oven-baked Pork Balls with Peppers.

There is absolutely no need to forego beef when cooking on a budget. This section provides a range of recipes using mince but also ones using cheaper cuts of beef cooked to be meltingly tasty. Choose from homely and traditional dishes such as Cottage Pie or Steak and Kidney Stew, or go for a Goan-style Beef Curry.

Just like beef, lamb can be delicious at very affordable prices – it simply depends on how you cook it, and there are many ways. Whether you go for a slow-cooked treat such as Braised Lamb with Broad Beans, or exploit the less popular parts of the animal such as in Tagliatelle with Creamy Liver and Basil or Risotto with Lambs' Kidneys and Caramelised Shallots, you will eat a dish to remember.

Poultry can provide a lower-fat and more affordable alternative to red meat – it is especially good value for money if you buy with skin on, opt for thighs over breasts or go for turkey instead of chicken. A wide range of chicken and turkey recipes is suegsted here, from sticky Coriander Chicken and Soy Sauce Cakes to Cheesy Chicken Burgers that the kids will love.

Vegetables & Vegetarian

Vegetables top the list of value-for-money produce. They are cheaper than meat and fish and are essential for nutrition, not to mention their variety and taste. The savings continue if you buy in season – not forgetting that you will reduce your carbon footprint by not buying vegetables flown from faraway climes. Consequently you are spoilt for choice in this chapter, which includes such delights as Beetroot Risotto and Creamy Vegetable Korma.

Baking & Desserts

Baking your own bread clearly saves you money as well as filling your home with tantalising aromas, so we have included a recipe for Quick Brown Bread, as well as a Bacon and Tomato Breakfast Twist, which should be universally appealing. And counting the pennies does not have to translate to never treating yourself to dessert, so why not try our budget-friendly Fruity Roulade or Carrot Cake?

Index

Series Foreword

Last night I made a chorizo and chickpea casserole. I sweated some onions in a little olive oil, threw in the chopped-up Spanish sausage and, once it had released its golden, paprika-spiked juices, I added chicken stock, chickpeas and some sliced cabbage. It bubbled away happily for about 20 minutes, and then I finished it off with a squeeze of lemon juice and a bit of seasoning and ate it with a crust of bread. It probably cost a total of three pounds and was utterly delicious, even if I do say so myself.

Did I do it to be cheap? Not at all – although the fact that it didn't break the bank was certainly a bonus. I did it because that is what proper cooking is about – taking a few raw ingredients and, through the alchemy of heat, creating a dish that is greater than the sum of its parts.

People get too hung up on price anyway. Budget cooking doesn't necessarily mean cheap cooking. It doesn't mean filling your fridge with two-for-ones or limp vegetables going cheap at the market. It's more a state of mind, of being aware of what food is costing you and making the most of what you then buy. Sometimes I like to cook a beautiful steak or a whole sea bass, neither of which can be called cheap, but if I can wring maximum value out of them, it's money well spent.

Let's go back to that chorizo casserole. The most expensive element was the chorizo. I got mine from my local butcher so, while it wasn't authentically Spanish, it was half the price. I wouldn't serve it thinly sliced with an aperitif, but for throwing into a stew it was well up to the job. Why pay extra if you aren't going to appreciate its nuances of flavour? Ditto the olive oil – only a fool fries with extra virgin – save that for dressing a salad or finished dish.

The stock was home-made, using the carcass from a Sunday roast, plus the peelings from the leeks and carrots I served it with. That doesn't mean it was free, because, to make a decent stock, you need to start with a decent free-range chicken. But it meant I could justify buying the more expensive bird and enjoying its superior flavour, because I knew it would be giving me not one, but two meals.

So, spend your money where it counts, and plan ahead. These are the cornerstones of budget cooking. It's not about deprivation, but about that rather old-fashioned notion of good housekeeping. And finally, don't beat yourself up too much. I ended up using two cans of prepared chickpeas, when I should really have soaked my own the night before. But really, pre-soaking chickpeas? Who's got time for that?

Tony Turnbull is food and drink editor of *The Times*

Introduction

Even when we are not experiencing a massive global credit crunch, rising inflation, a reduction in lending or a squeeze on our spending and saving, shopping, planning and cooking for the family on a tight budget is a constant challenge for millions of people. And yet, believe it or not, it is perfectly possible to cook tasty, healthy and filling dishes for your family for under £5!

The £5 figure is a great objective to aim for, and you will find many recipes in this book that should come in under that, but first and foremost, it is important to learn how to buy food cheaply, cook economically and avoid wastage. There are many tips and skills to discover, but it will soon become second nature to shop within the household budget without restricting your family to a limited, boring or unhealthy diet.

Lessons from Our Forebears

Thankfully, we are not in unfamiliar territory. There are millions of people alive today around the world who lived through the Great Depression, the Second World War and the post-war gloom. They too had large families to feed, bills to pay and a tight budget on which to live. And they did survive, showing great resourcefulness in the way they shopped, grew their own, cooked and stored their food.

This book is not advocating a return to the 1940s, to a time of powdered eggs, reusing old teabags and borrowing a cup of sugar from your neighbour. What we are advocating is considering the resourcefulness of our forebears, who made the most of the little they had, and looking at ways to apply some of these handy hints and tips to our own individual situations.

For example, with a bit of practice, families need never buy any more stocks, soups, pastes or preserves because they can grow, cook, prepare and store them themselves. Even 50 years ago, it was considered a luxury to buy your soups or preserves. Recipes dredged up from the inter-war years and the Second World War celebrations show just how easy it really is to cook some of these things from scratch.

An Arsenal of Cost-saving Techniques

There are modern ways to make savings, too. The internet has brought with it a host of opportunity at our fingertips: the ability to compare and contrast prices and discounts on offer at various supermarkets; information on how to grow and store our own fresh produce; and useful ideas to help us save electricity and gas when cooking the family meal, for example.

So, there is no need to restrict your family to low-cost, high-fat convenience food. Throw the ready meals out of the window and say hello to home-made meals that the whole household will enjoy – we can feed our families on what seems to be an ever-tightening household spend. Let this book be a motivation to stop worrying about where the money will come from, and start making great plans to provide good meals for your family the best you can, no matter how tight the budget becomes.

Shopping & Cooking on a Budget

Setting the Budget

Your budget is not always going to be as simple as £5 per meal – that does not include snacks or small meals, for example. Before setting out to go food shopping, it is important to set a budget that you will not excede – but it must be realistic. Families often set unrealistically small targets, which can cause further monetary problems.

Working Out How Much You Can Spend

Obviously this depends on your income, and how much is left over after paying off all those other family bills: heating, energy, travel, mortgage and school fees. Official research statistics prove that families are finding it increasingly difficult to meet food costs: you are not alone if you are wondering how to make ends meet. But even assuming that there is a little left in the barrel after the mortgage and other bills are paid, you also have to be realistic about how much your family shop comes to. How can you gauge what is essential expenditure?

Keep Your Till Receipts

By keeping till receipts, families can look back at, say, three months' worth of receipts and work out what the average spend should be. This can be important in setting your food budget for the year ahead. Here are some benefits of doing this:

- **Price rises**: You can see which foodstuffs have risen in price. This will help you decide whether a different store might work out to be better value.

- **Not-so-little extras**: You can see how much 'extra' and unplanned food items cost. This will help you stick to your shopping list (see 'Planning the Shop', page 19) and avoid shelling out for items you did not consider in the budget plan.

- **What do you not eat?** Looking at the receipts, are there any food items you buy that your family does not really eat? Have you just got into the habit of buying six bottles of milk a week, when in fact you only really need four?

- **The average spend**: Shopping bills can help you work out an average spend and can help you think about keeping within a certain band. By cutting out the unnecessary and the unplanned, you could set a reasonable budget, setting an upper and lower limit for flexibility, for each week. You will save money immediately if you stick within that band.

- **Checking supermarkets**: Comparing receipts from different stores will indicate where to shop for the best prices on your family staples such as cereal, bread, juice and meat. It is not just about comparing random prices across each store to see who has got the highest number of discounts, but looking at what your family actually buys and whether this research can help lower your budget.

Think Ahead for Special Occasions

If you know you have a family birthday or celebration coming up, make sure you factor this extra expenditure into your budget. Either set up a separate cash account way in advance to save for this expenditure, or make a sensible budget plan for that week's food spend.

Spend As Much As Your Family Eats

No more, no less! Do not cut back so much that meals are insufficient. But do not over-estimate what your family can eat. A filling, healthy meal can be provided within a sensible budget.

Waste Not, Want Not

If you over-estimate the spend, you will be tempted to use up the full amount, probably on over-priced snack foods or stuff that will only get thrown away. Even in 2008, according to the World Food Programme, consumers in the US, UK and Western Europe were wasting 30 per cent of food purchased. In the US alone, this was worth an estimated US$48.3bn.

Ways Not to Waste

Thinking about what tends to get wasted in your household will help you work out what to buy and what not to buy. Here are some things to help you get started:

- **Forgotten fridge items**: What tends to get left in the fridge until it has curdled its way past its use-by date? Yogurts? Pickles? Cut back on buying it.

- **Timing is everything**: Does your family tend to eat more at lunchtime and only want a little to eat in the evening? Then do not buy loads of ingredients for big evening meals, as these are likely to linger until they are thrown out.

- **Only buy what you want**: Buying more than you need means too much waste food at the end of the week.

- **Bake it, don't fake it**: Do you buy several cakes (on the insistence of your eight-year-old) that only get half-eaten?

Why not just buy the bare ingredients for baking a cake? It will save money in the long term and provide something fun to do together as a family.

Weekly or Monthly Budget?

Those who get paid weekly, or who do not own a car, may find that a smaller, weekly shop is better. In this case, work out how much you can set aside each week for spending, and apportion some of that to the food shop. There are two main advantages of weekly rather than monthly shopping:

 Reducing waste: You will naturally reduce wastage, as you are more likely to use up all the food that you have bought; people who shop monthly often leave food to go past its use-by date.

 Cash is king: Weekly shoppers may be more likely to use cash to pay for their groceries, so this keeps them within their set budget; it is easy to go overboard when you are carrying around a credit or debit card.

Card Caution

If you shop monthly, you are less likely to carry around a significant wad of cash in your wallet and are more likely to pay by card. This can be risky. Make sure that you are not tempted to bust your budget because you have the 'freedom' to do so on your credit or debit card. By the same token, avoid buying too much food that will only get wasted simply because you can. In both instances, the point is to stick within a reasonable, achievable budget and to see where you can shave off unnecessary expenses.

Where Do Your Priorities Lie?

It may be very difficult for you to make a regular budget. Perhaps you are self-employed or working on a contract-only basis, or you have debt problems. If there is only a certain amount left in the kitty and your average monthly shop is at least four times that amount, you either try to make do on what you have (which might be an unrealistic expectation, considering the number of people in the family) or you sort out what other expenditures you have been laying out that require attention. You have to eat to live.

Ask Yourself How to Prioritise

By taking time to go through your finances at the start of the month, you will find you can set aside the right amount to cover important costs, such as the family food budget, without getting further into debt or cutting back so far that you end up with beans for supper every night.

- **Eat out less**: Perhaps you could go out less and put more food on the table?

- **Rearrange or pay off your loans**: Do you need to sort out your loan arrangements so that you do not have to shell out such high rates of interest on repayments?

Who Can Help with Financial Planning?

In these recessionary times, it is important to get some specialist advice to help out if you are really struggling. Possible sources of help are:

- **Bank**: A personal representative at your bank should be able to give you some free budgeting advice.

- **Independent financial adviser**: If you pay a fee, as opposed to commission, you should get completely impartial advice on your situation. The internet offers various ways of searching for a qualified adviser in your area.

- **Your accountant**: If you have your own accountant, make use of them!

- **A debt specialist**: You can contact a debt specialist at a free, charity-based service such as Mind or the Citizens Advice Bureau.

Planning the Shop

So, you have your budget sorted out and decided whether you tend to shop monthly or weekly. Now it comes to planning ahead. This is the best way to save money and stick within your budget – and it really takes no time at all! We are not talking about a military-style attitude towards family meals, but taking a couple of minutes to think ahead about what you need could save you a lot of money.

Making a List

Making a list sounds like something your granny does for a hobby, but it is really important. How many times have you come back from the supermarket without the toilet rolls or washing-up liquid? How many times have you, instead, bought six or seven items that you did not need, just because you were not sure whether you needed them or not?

Tips for Compiling

Instead of rushing at the last minute to make a list of things you need to get, or not bothering at all and picking up anything you see, try the following:

 The till receipts:
Use your last few shopping bills as a

basis for remembering certain items and working out which supermarkets could offer the best price on your family essentials.

✓ **Who ate the last cookie?** Take note of 'empties' during the week. Why not keep a magnetic notepad on the fridge and train yourself (and your family) to write down when they finish an item?

✓ **Running on empty:** Make a note of everyday items that are running low, especially those items which might not be as widely available in many supermarkets. These might be things such as special soya milk or gluten-free bread.

✓ **Keep the coupons handy:** If you have particular money-off coupons, or have saved up loyalty points or stamps, make sure that you keep these with the list, in your wallet or purse, ready for the big shop.

Branded for Life

How many times have you or a family member bought the wrong brand or flavour of something, only for it to sit on the shelf until it gets thrown away? Keeping a list can also help you remember which brand and type of food went down well with the family, and which brands were met with general disapproval. This will help reduce unnecessary spending and keep your household budget low.

Planning the Weekly Meals

If you have a rough plan in your head for what the week has in store in terms of meals, you will save money by being able to include the appropriate components in your list. This is because you will have what you need and will not have to rush out last-minute to a more expensive local or convenience store; you can gauge quantities more precisely, so you do not end up buying more than you need; you can figure out where to go for the best deals on certain food items you need for various meals; and, if you are going to have guests over for dinner one night, you can think ahead to make the most of any bargains or bulk-buy discounts.

When to Shop?

We all lead busy lives, so it is no wonder that the majority of us pile down to the nearest supermarket on a Saturday or Sunday in order to get in the weekly or monthly groceries. But this can lead to a quick dash round a crowded supermarket, with fractious children and hungry teenagers loitering wistfully around the freshly-baked cookies counter. Being stressed leads to the famous phrase: 'Let's just get out of here as quickly as possible', which can lead to picking up the first thing you see, rather than having the time to compare prices or search for the best bargains.

The Early Bird Catches the Worm

Why not get up a little earlier and shop when there are fewer people around and a clearer car park? You will have more leisure to follow your list and pick up more bargains along the way.

Evening Advantages

Or, if you can shop later on in the evening, and especially on a weekday, you will not only find that it is not so crowded and you have time to think, but you will also find that many supermarkets do discounts on big-ticket items towards the end of the day. And individual stores will set their own end-of-line bargain prices, which you will not see if you go online to compare stores. But remember, cheap does not mean necessary: do not be misled into thinking that because it is a 'bargain', you must need it. If it is not on the list, do not buy it.

Where to Shop?

In a busy world where we are cash-strapped and time-poor, it is difficult to make the right choices about where to shop. The local convenience store may be nearby and open all hours, but it probably costs significantly more than the supermarket that is 20 minutes' drive away. However, for some families, if they do not have a car, or if there is just one parent, who has to work, the convenience store can be the easiest and default option. But how do you tell who has the best bargains?

Online Shopping

Shops are also recognising that many people do not have the ability or time to do big weekly or monthly shops in store. Many supermarkets now offer online shopping, complete with door-to-door delivery, which can benefit you if you are unable to get to the shops physically, do not have the time to go or are likely to spend as much on petrol as on delivery

User-friendly

Busy mother-of-two Misha Sergeant, from Leicester, says, 'When I'm just not able to get out to the shops, I find that internet shopping is quite a good way of making sure you only get what you need. As you look at the various items in your virtual basket, you can review the list and add on anything you have forgotten. Also, I have often got up, looked in

my fridge and cupboards to see what I needed, then gone back to the computer and added these to the basket... and taken away things I didn't really need.'

Ask If There Are Any Discounts

Many of these delivery sites will have special delivery discounts and concessions for those who are elderly or have a disability, while others will offer 'extras' to boost online ordering.

Price Comparison on the Internet

A quick search for 'best prices for food shopping' will throw up a host of comparison websites, useful chat forums and even blogs that can help you compare prices. Some websites have updates to let you know which stores have recently discounted certain ranges and which stores are offering the best prices on certain foodstuffs, so you can get a pretty good picture of where you might be able to save money. Some sites claim that you can save between 20 and 30 per cent on your average family food shop. So, even if you do not intend to *buy* online, the internet can help you save money on your shop.

Price Comparison Websites

There are some websites, such as www.mysupermarket.co.uk, that enable you to automatically compare specific food prices in competing superstores. Some food shopping price comparison websites take you all the way through to purchasing your items, so you don't have to go to the actual store's website separately.

Earn Points and Find the Best Prices

Some price comparison sites have a loyalty scheme where you can gain virtual points with them as well as the usual points you will get with your specific supermarket on your store loyalty or club card. These virtual points can be traded at other sites for a variety of goods, days out or gifts. Also, some websites will show daily deals and best prices on a range of products at each supermarket. So, regardless of whether you want to swap supermarkets or not, you can see at a glance where the best prices are.

Deals of the Week

Each supermarket will feature its latest deals on its own website, whether weekly or daily. It is worth taking a peek at your store's website before you go shopping; if you have time, look at the nearest rival's website too, to see just what is on offer.

Discount Stores

The well-established brand-name superstores are facing stiff – and increasingly public – competition from non-domestic, self-proclaimed 'hypermarkets' such as Aldi, Lidl and Netto. Offering significant discounts to the big-name rivals, these are springing up all over the UK and starting to make inroads into North America. While other food giants are cutting jobs and closing stores, these newer discount stores are growing in popularity. They are able to do this through a mixture of bulk buying, low overheads through less attractive stores, not giving free bags, fewer staff and cutting it finer when it comes to use-by dates.

Are They Really Always Cheaper?

There are many surveys online that can help to gauge whether or not these stores really do offer better value for money. This is based not just on the number of food items sold at a lower price, but also the quality and the quantity (for example, whether the bulk buys offer a better saving in a cheaper outlet than a no-name or own-brand bulk buy in a 'domestic' store). A simple Google search will throw up some of these websites.

Which Foods Are Cheaper in These Stores?

The answer may be 'pretty much everything'. Food that is generally cheaper than in a standard supermarket includes:

 meat
 cheese (significantly so)
 bulk-buy pastas, noodles, rice
 loose vegetables (check the freshness, though)

snack foods

 frozen 'finger food' for parties

 traditional Christmas or other seasonal food

 cartons of fruit juice

 cans of fruit or pie and pastry filling

 four- and six-pack cans of soup, beans or pasta shapes (half the price)

Open Your Mind

Do not be put off by the fact that labels may be primarily in Spanish, German or Polish — most have translations into English. Many of these discounted items are leading brands in Mexico, Germany or Spain, similar to the leading brands in 'domestic' stores. Do not assume that it cannot be any good because it is an unfamiliar brand. You may find that it tastes better and is even healthier.

The Farmers' Market

These are more popular in rural areas but are starting to make inroads into the cities thanks to the rising popularity of organic and free-range food. Markets are sometimes bypassed in this busy age of instant consumerism, but the experience is great, as is the potential for best-price bargains on fresh and home-made food. With a little careful planning, you can find out where the local markets are each week

or month, and perhaps going to a farmers' market might become a nice day out for the family once a month.

What Can You Get?

Although you cannot get a lot of the items you may buy in bulk from the supermarkets, such as cans and other non-perishables, there is still a wide range of produce available from farmers' markets (not to mention non-food items such as crafts), including fresh meat and meat produce, cheeses, sauces, pickles, syrups and jams, home-made wines and cordials, bread, cakes and pastries, home-grown vegetables and fruit, and dairy produce.

Are They Cheaper?

A farmers' market is not always cheaper, but they offer a different choice of produce to supermarkets, and more organic and ethically produced foods. And there are some savings to be had at farmers' markets:

- **Organic savings**: Superstores usually charge higher fees on organic meat than you would pay for the same quality at a farmers' market.

- **Try before you buy**: You can taste before you buy, which means that if you do not like it, you do not have to buy it, unlike a supermarket where you have to buy first and thus risk wasting food.

- **Negotiation**: Many of the farmers will do deals or haggle a price with you for bulk buys, so do not go by price tags alone.

The Traditional Market

Because many of these stallholders will import their food directly, they are not subject to the same tax restrictions as the supermarkets are. Plus, they want to sell off their goods at the end of the day because they do not have the storage – so competing cheaply on volume is the way to do it. Finally, the overheads a market trader will have to pay are very low compared with the bills a store has to face.

Different Tastes

Immigration has done a wonderful thing in injecting new life into the flagging marketplaces of cities. It has brought new tastes and food ideas to the fore and has found a willing audience of people wanting to try new things without having to pay the higher prices that a supermarket will front-load on to the goods.

Fruit and Veg

There are several advantages at markets when it comes to fruit and vegetables:

By weight, not unit: Because market stalls charge according to weight, you will save money by getting just the right portions you want, without wasting any.

Exotic competition: Some exotic fruits, such as mangoes, pineapples, yams and plantains are far cheaper in markets or local grocery stores than in supermarkets.

You do not pay for packaging: Try this challenge – buy a packet of tomatoes from a supermarket and the same number of fresh ones loose from a market stall. The market stall's local produce will usually work out to be the best price for (usually) fresher goods.

Organic food: You will not pay supermarket prices for buying fresh, home-grown, organic produce from a local marketplace.

Fishmongers and Butchers

Sometimes it is best to cut out the middleman and go straight to the wholesalers. Superstores do not offer you the full range of meat cuts or always show you the best fish dishes to fit your family budget. Many people wrongly assume that a butcher or fishmonger is going to be more expensive as you pay a premium for the freshest meat, or that, because he is a smallholding, his higher overheads will be passed on to you. However, you could save a significant amount by learning how to cook some of the more unusual cuts available at butchers and also learn how to make your family meals more varied, healthy and exciting.

A Meaty Difference

While supermarket-bought meat is convenient and cleanly packed, there are certain things to watch out for with meat in supermarkets:

 The 'water' load: Many shops will inject water into meat to help it freeze. So when they weigh meat, some stores will not take into account the water load and will charge you for both the meat and the water therein. The water, of course, evaporates in the cooking process, meaning you actually got less for your money.

 Actual weight v. price: Also, while on the subject of weight, bear in mind that many weight-based prices fluctuate significantly on products such as cheese or meat, but the actual difference in terms of what you get to serve up on your plate is not always as great as the price may lead you to believe. For example, a pack of eight lamb chops might vary 'by weight' by as much as 50p. But will that variation make a difference to what your family will eat? Probably not – so get the cheaper option.

Variety: A wholesale butcher or fishmonger at a market, or a local butcher's store, will have a wider range of cuts and often offer lower prices. A supermarket, because of space constraints, might not always devote shelf space to a wider (and potentially cheaper) range of cuts.

 In-house butchers: Even if you do go to the butcher's counter at a supermarket, remember that, while you are getting fresh, quality-assured meat and a slightly wider range of cuts (for example, you will get liver and kidneys here), he is still there to raise money for the superstore and may not always offer you the cheapest cut each time.

Specialist Stores

Most supermarkets offer food from around the world to cater for increasingly diverse tastes. But there are also many independent shops and delicatessens that can offer more choice for your money. Just because they look specialist does not mean that they will charge you specialist prices. They are worth a look.

General Stores

Sometimes it is worth buying on impulse when it comes to looking for savings for the family. General stores such as Poundland, The Pound Shop or 99p Stores, to name just a few, may not primarily be food stores as they stock all sorts of products, but they may be the source of some surprise deals. If you see a deal in an unexpected place, and you know your family usually buys such items, then it is worth picking up the deal and crossing it off the shopping list. Just remember not to be fooled by the bright stickers stating that everything in the store is £1 – sometimes the foodstuff is cheaper in supermarkets. Quality-wise, too, some of the no-brand cheap chocolates, wines and champagnes are not worth buying. Not everything is a best buy just because it is in a cheap store.

Tactics and Offers

There are all sorts of ways to improve your chances of getting the best deals when food shopping. There are so many kinds of offers or discounts and there are many pitfalls to be wary of. By doing all you can to shop wisely, you will find the best bargains and meet your budget.

Reduced to Clear

Most leading supermarkets will have a range of heavily discounted foodstuffs that are approaching the end of their shelf life. It is also worth asking if you might have a discount on damaged goods. However, remember the difference between the different dates on produce: a use-by date really means it is the end of a product's life, a best-before date is a guideline (sometimes a foodstuff is good for a week after the best-before date) and a sell-by date is an arbitrary measure telling staff when to replenish stock on the shelves (although the food may be good for a week or so yet).

Special Offers

There are all sorts of special deals around: 'buy-one-get-one-free' ('BOGOF') or 'two-for-one' ('2-4-1'), '25 per cent off (or extra)', 'three-for-the-price-of-two' and special half-price lures are becoming a mainstay in supermarkets throughout the year. This sort of deal is great if you really need what is being offered. It is worth planning this strategically, but do not get carried away. Here are some pointers on how to treat special offers:

Look for Deals on the Family Staples

If you have the freezer space and you see deals on milk, bread, sausages, bacon and so on, then buy them and save them. This is particularly good for meat and higher-ticket items.

Be Alert

However, there are some things to watch
out for, as not every deal may be the best
bargain-buy for your family. There have
been investigations by various consumer
watchdogs about deals such as 2-4-1.
They discovered that, while the special
offer price takes into account the fact that

two items are being sold for the price of one, the price of 'one' is somewhat nominal and has
been found to have been raised when used as part of a buy-one-get-one-free deal. While the
cost per item is proportionately cheaper than if bought on its own, it is not actually half price,
critics claim. So be canny about your purchases.

Extra Free?

25 per cent (or 50 per cent) 'extra' free has also generated flurries of customer letters claiming
that stores and manufacturers sometimes put up the price of a product before coming out
with a short-term 25 per cent extra free offer. Other consumer champions have seen that the
packaging may look a lot larger to entice consumers but, weight-for-weight, another cereal
may be offering a better price.

Watch Your Budget

Finally, just because it is a special deal, if it is not on your usual shopping list, do not buy it.
It will only break the family food budget – show willpower!

Own Brands and Basics Brands

Many people like to stick to their well-known brands of pizza or pasta, whether out of habit
or because of certain allergies or intolerances. However, leaving aside those who need
to use certain brands because of health issues, breaking the habit of always buying the
most expensive brand-name goods can save you a lot of money on your household

shopping budget. There is an increasingly wide range of own-brand and no-brand, or 'basics', goods: you can get everything from pasta and margarine to feminine care and toothpaste. Look around for where the deals are to be found. You will be surprised at how much you can get for a lot less when you start to switch from the big-name brands to your store's own brand.

Busting the Brand Myth

Here are a few more pointers to encourage you to save money on your family's average food spend:

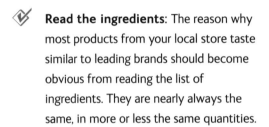 **Read the ingredients**: The reason why most products from your local store taste similar to leading brands should become obvious from reading the list of ingredients. They are nearly always the same, in more or less the same quantities.

Taste testing: When eggs, flour, raisins or butter from a store's own-brand range of food is mixed together into a cake, it is very hard for anyone to tell the difference between the own-brand ingredients and the leading brand names.

Fruit and vegetables: Sometimes there are ranges of packaged fruit and vegetables: a premium brand, the store's own brand and its basic or value-brand fruit or vegetables. There is little difference in the taste, particularly when cooked in a casserole.

Beware of the 'Budget Blinkers'

Don't get so caught up in buying the basics or value, no-frills range that you miss out on good offers on branded goods. Also, try not to let your mission for the cheapest food obscure any ethical considerations – for example buying free-range eggs instead of eggs from battery or caged hens.

Making the Most of Deals and Offers

In addition to the 2-4-1s, do not forget to get as much as you can out of coupons, points and other deals, as well as your loyalty cards.

Junk Mail

Do not throw away any marketing that comes through your door before you have checked it. There may be some discount coupons that may be useful. Keep them in your purse.

Look Online

Sometimes money-off vouchers can be found on independent websites or the store's own website. You can print these off and use them against certain items. Beware, though; not all the vouchers may be for everyone to use. The same applies to discount delivery codes, which are internet codes that can cut the price of home shopping.

Take a Raincheck

Ask for what are commonly called 'raincheck' vouchers – if a special offer item is not in stock, the store manager might give you a voucher entitling you to the same deal at a later date.

Points Promotions

In-store deals offering extra points for a particular product are a great way to save for that rainy day or big celebration.

Surveys

If you are offered the chance to win free shopping for a year just by filling in a survey, then go for it. What have you got to lose? Or, what could you gain?

Making the Most of Your Loyalty Cards

You are earning points, so make the most of them by spending them to defray the cost of your shopping every now and then. If you can collect Air Miles on these cards, even better – your food shopping could help to pay for your holiday to Florida.

Starting to Cook

With most families finding that they need two salaries to live on in these credit-crunch times, it is becoming more of a chore to think about cooking a meal every night. It is no surprise that many people opt for a takeaway, ready meal or the convenience store for their nightly dinner. Plus, with many families working on shift patterns, teenagers out or hibernating in their rooms for much of the evening, planning and preparing the family meal can be almost impossible. Almost, but not quite.

Working out Quantities

Singledom is the best time to learn to cook, but it cannot prepare you for the onslaught of getting family meals ready each day. Even assuming that everyone in the house likes and can eat the same food (which would be a miracle), the sheer quantities of food involved can be mind-boggling.

Cooking with Bulk Items

Having saved money by buying family-sized packs or bulk items such as noodles, frozen peas or rice, it is sometimes tempting to use a little more of these than we should in each meal, because the bag or packet looks never-ending. Here is a secret – it is not. It will run out sooner than you think, unless you are careful.

Don't Just Use It Up

If you think there is only a little bit of a certain ingredient left, you might be tempted to throw it all in. Don't. It will only get wasted. Try making it into something, such as a soup or stuffing.

Never Over-estimate

Too often we are not convinced that a certain amount of food will be enough per person. But think about the various appetites: small children and older people will not eat huge portions. Try the following:

- **Measure it out!** Until you get used to cooking a certain dish so that you can automatically gauge the right amount, use measuring cups, scales and jugs to help you get the right portion per person.

- **Make a fist**: This should be the size of a portion of noodles, mashed potato or rice to accompany a meal for an adult.

- **Count the carrots**: Assume, as a rough rule of thumb, that half a carrot should be apportioned per person as part of a wider meal. Apply the same rule to parsnips, celery, courgettes and aubergines.

- **Divvy up the potatoes**: When doing roasts, count the prepared potatoes in the pan and allocate a certain even number to each person (usually between four and six). Someone will always want more or less so it balances out.

Working from Recipes

This is the easiest way to gauge how much food you will need to prepare per person. Recipes enable you to:

- **Plan the shop**: Do you need more chicken than you have in the freezer, for instance?

- **Conduct mental swaps**: Work out what to replace certain ingredients with so that you can use what you have, rather than buy new things.

- **Think about portion allocation**: Estimate how much each family member can eat.

Think about leftovers: You will be able to gauge whether you will have enough left over for someone's lunch the next day.

Trial and Error

If you are not working from a recipe, or the recipe resulted in too much or too little, you will learn from trial and error. If you have not baked enough lasagne one day, for example, make a note of it and increase the amounts you use the next time. If you have made too much food, write down what tends to get half-eaten or left on plates and cook less of it next time.

Time Matters

It is no wonder people grab a takeaway, open a ready-made pasta packet or bung a ready meal into the microwave. We live in a fast-paced world and while we might enjoy cooking when there is time, we often find ourselves pressed for time: work, family and other commitments all crowd in. But it *is* possible to stop buying the convenience food and the ready-made sauces and start saving money while not adding to our stress levels.

The Kitchen Time Lord

Students eating at weird hours of the day, working adults coming home late and children leaving school early and demanding to be fed immediately: all these can take the stuffing out of the person preparing the food. And if we are not careful, this will take the stuffing out of our budget as well. So try not to keep people waiting too long for their meal or they will snack, but also remember to work in small stages so you do not have to do too many things at once.

A Step in Time

Knowing in advance when people will get up and come back home is a starting point. Of course, this involves communication, but preparing home-cooked meals and snacks will save lots of money, helping the family not to rely on takeaways or quick-fix ready meals, while getting them involved, however old they are.

Stretching Meals

There is a lot to be said for leftovers! And meals can go further than you think. This section looks more in depth at how to make a meal out of just a few ingredients, using leftovers in resourceful ways, avoiding wastage and making your own so you do not have to spend lots of money buying items such as sauces and stocks.

Making a Meal Go Further

If you are running low on ingredients, there is no need to rush for the nearest store to stock up. Take a look around at what you do have first, as this will save you time and money.

Thicken it Up!

If you are cooking a casserole or stew, but do not think there is enough meat or prime ingredient to go round, thicken it up with peas, lentils, rice, sweetcorn, potatoes or pasta shapes.

Short on Vegetables...

If you do not have enough vegetables to accompany a meal, instead of buying new ones, think about making them up into a 'sauce' by adding a little stock and ketchup, some chopped tomatoes or some tomato soup.

... Long on Staples?

Do not just add more staple food to the plate to make it look like there is more food! Think about how to make it more interesting – it could be as simple as adding caraway seeds and black beans to rice, or mashing onion, mustard or leftover broccoli into mashed potatoes.

Be Bold

Be willing to try adding new or different ingredients, but please account for tastes:

- **Low on minced/ground beef?** Try bulking up your bolognese sauce with a little sausage or chopped ham.

- **Running low on cheese?** Make a herby white sauce to cover the cauliflower or macaroni, and then grate the small piece of cheese on top of the dish before cooking.

- **Thicken soups**: Add puréed potato (boil it up and blend it to a pulp) to soups and broths to thicken them.

- **Oaty crumble topping**: Mix oats and flour to create crumble toppings if you are low on flour.

- **Improve pizzas**: Jazz up plain pizzas with leftover pepper, tomatoes and sweetcorn.

New Dishes from Leftovers

You can always find ways to use those 'little bits' left over for the whole family to enjoy, rather than have one person eating them up or, worse, throwing them away. Waste not, want not... Here are some examples:

Bubble 'n' Squeak

A classic for brunch or a light dinner, this uses odds and ends of potato, vegetables and meat, all bound together with egg and fried (you can use low-fat oil instead of the traditional lard!). All the ingredients, except for the egg, should have been cooked beforehand. Simply dice the cold meat and vegetables, beat the eggs (allowing one egg per person) and then stir them into the meat and vegetables. Fry over a moderate heat for 10–15 minutes, turning after 5 minutes.

Rissoles

Another wartime classic, rissoles are a brilliant way of using leftovers without making your family groan with boredom. These can be made using any leftover cooked meat or veg, and will stretch a small amount of food. Simply dice the meat or veg and set aside, then, in a pan, make a white sauce from any leftover gravy or stock (made up with 300 ml/½ pt milk), some seasoning and 1 heaped tablespoon flour. After it boils, add the meat, spread it on to a plate, cool it down and add breadcrumbs. Shape it how you like, let it set for a while, then fry it up.

Meat Paste

This was popular in the interwar period during the 1920s and 1930s, and was used on toast, or as a cheap pâté with cheese, crackers and quince. Simply take the remainder of any cooked meat, mince it finely, add some herbs and spices and push through a sieve. Mix it together with 50 g/2 oz butter and put it into jars, pouring a little melted butter over the top to seal in the flavour.

Vegetable or Meat Timbales

Using leftover minced/ground meat, canned ham or corn, or roast vegetables, this is very similar to rissoles, only it is steamed instead of being fried. Blend the meat or vegetables together with 25 g/1 oz breadcrumbs, 1 egg and some herbs. Make up a white sauce (see below for instructions) and mix this into the ingredients, along with salt and pepper. Pour the mixture into greased moulds and steam for 20–30 minutes. Serve with a small helping of plain pasta, lightly tossed with oil and parsley.

Multiple Remixes

There are so many ways to make each of the dishes above, and there are many more dinners that can be made out of what is left over. The objective of the cooks of yesteryear, who came up with the idea of turning one day's meal into another completely different one, was to prevent boredom as much as to protect the food budget. Nobody wants to eat the same thing two days in a row; with careful planning and a little bit of panache, easy dishes can stretch the leftover food into a delicious meal the following day without stretching your bank account.

One Day's Dinner is the Next Day's Lunch

Well, not necessarily the next day – you have the option of storing and saving it for a day or so later, for when you feel like it. But however you want to mix it up for variety, the fact remains that if you use leftovers wisely, you will save a lot of money by not having to spend on expensive lunches. Even if you would 'only' spend a few pounds on lunch each day, if you do it every day for five days, this works out at quite a significant potential saving in the working week. Multiply that by 52 and you could knock a staggering sum off your yearly food budget.

Bake and Freeze

By making a little more than you would eat one day, you can save the remaining food for another. For example, suppose you bake a lasagne for six people, accompanied with salad or vegetables, but you are a family of four. You might have enough for two whole adult portions left over, which you could freeze together or separately. This could become two days' worth of lunch, or a light meal another evening.

The Cold Roast Sandwich

Everyone knows the famous turkey sandwich, made the day after Christmas with the leftover turkey meat and stuffing. But why not apply this 'rule' to every roast meal that you have? Doing this means that you will not need to throw away the leftover cuts of meat if there were only a few remaining post-roast; nor will you have to store a small amount in the fridge or freezer. Most importantly, you will save money by avoiding lunchtime purchases and spending less on sandwich fillers.

Sad Salad

If you have had a salad the night before and there is only a dribble left, do not throw it out. It could be used in a sandwich, to garnish a baked potato, or bolstered up with a little more lettuce and chopped tomato and made into a light lunch the next day. Remember, the more you save, the less you need to buy – and the less you need to buy, the healthier your budget will be.

Soups, Stocks and Sauces

It is shocking when we consider how much we pay for shop-bought meat or pasta sauces, canned soups, condiments and stock. Yet all these things can be made really cheaply with the ingredients we already have – and are using without knowing it – when we cook. They are really easy as well, so why do we not do it more often instead of spending? Here are just a few ideas to help you make your own and cut out a significant portion of your household food budget.

Apple Sauce

Apples that are going a little, well, wrinkly, are no good to eat but they *are* good for sauces and cooking. Instead of throwing them out, wash, peel, chop and boil them up with a little sugar and water and you have ready-made chunky apple sauce that can be used in pies, crumbles, preserves and to accompany pork.

Resourceful Salad Dressings

Many families buy salad dressing that only gets used once or twice, then is left to go mouldy in the fridge drawer. This is a waste and will damage the budget. But it is possible to make your own while using up the odds and ends of other jars and bottles. You need: the last bit of Dijon mustard, the remnants of the vinegar bottle and a scoop of honey (or whatever is left in the old jar). Mix them all together with a little warm boiled water and you have a honey and mustard salad dressing.

White Sauce

Rather than buying expensive packet mixes or jars of white sauces, make them yourself by stirring a little flour into a saucepan with some melted butter and whisking in some milk, little by little, until it has all blended but not boiled. Stir continuously. This is a basic white sauce, to which you could add pepper, if liked. To make it béchamel sauce, add some grated nutmeg and a little cream, or to make it cheese sauce, add some grated cheese and some herbs. To save on milk, use milk diluted with vegetable water.

Cheat's Soup

If you have not got enough leftovers for a sufficient portion for another meal, or even for bubble and squeak or rissoles, make the leftovers into a soup with the addition of lentils to thicken it into a hearty broth. Serve with cheese on toast. See the soups section for some ideas.

Pasta Sauce

This is great for lasagnes and uses up lots of bits of vegetable. If you have a sausage or piece of ham left over from a previous meal, chop this into tiny pieces, together with half a grated carrot and half a grated celery stick. You do not need wine. Add half an onion, fry the sausage or ham in a little oil, then add the onion and the rest of the grated vegetables. When they are starting to brown, add 150 g/5 oz minced/ground beef (you can buy basic or no-frills for this) and, when this is browned, add a large tin of tomatoes and some dried herbs. You can simmer this on a low heat for 40 minutes or in a slow cooker.

Vegetarian Spaghetti Bolognese Sauce

Chop up an old half or whole onion and brown in a frying pan in a little light cooking oil, then add a large tin of chopped tomatoes and any tomatoes that are looking a little over-ripe, some dried herbs and any bits of bell pepper or other vegetables that you have left in your fridge. Simmer and season with (vegetarian) Worcestershire sauce, or similar, to taste.

Make Your Own Stock

Stock is the liquid obtained when bones, meat, fish or vegetables have been simmered in water to extract the flavour. It is the basis of most soups, sauces, stews and gravies. So, instead of spending on packaged stock cubes or (worse) jars of sauce or gravy, make your own in typical 1930s style: the water in which meat, rice or vegetables have been boiled may be substituted for stock, so, if the household is large, a stockpot should be kept in the fridge, into which should be put all suitable scraps such as vegetable peelings, tomato skins, meat trimmings and leftover scraps – avoid starchy food such as potatoes as this makes it cloudy. Boil it up, skim off any fat, strain and use. If you are keeping it for more than a day, boil it up each day.

Maximise the Meal, Minimise the Spend

Hopefully, this has given you more of an idea about how to use up the leftovers without resorting to throwing them out. It is not about using up the scraps left over on people's plates, but about what is left in the pots after serving up the right portions for each person and making the most of the little bits and bobs in your fridge and cupboards to maximise your meals and minimise your spend. For more ideas, check out www.lovefoodhatewaste.com.

Challenge: Meals For Under a Fiver

Recently, a national supermarket chain has been advertising ways that a family of four can cook a meal for just £5. But even if this can be done, can it include extras such as dessert? Does it have to be completely done from scratch? And can families buy food for the week and generate interesting meals each day, without resorting to the seemingly cheap yet very unhealthy option of opening a couple of pizza boxes?

The Simple Answer...

... is yes. It can include desserts (see the case study on the Appleyards at the end of this section), it does not always have to be done from scratch each time and it is not difficult for families to budget for a series of interesting meals that do not require a huge number of ingredients.

Versatile Ingredients

When buying and planning the meals, always think about food that can be used in several different ways. This will help you if you want to buy in bulk – how many dishes can you create using that one bulk packet of a certain food item? Thinking about the versatility of ingredients can really help you cut back on the number of different food items that you buy, which will reduce your budget significantly.

Versatile Staples

If you have a range of basic staple ingredients, you can chop and change and be prepared to be as flexible as possible within given time limits. Staples can be used in the following ways:

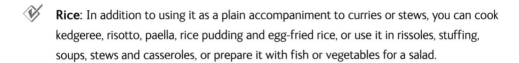

 Rice: In addition to using it as a plain accompaniment to curries or stews, you can cook kedgeree, risotto, paella, rice pudding and egg-fried rice, or use it in rissoles, stuffing, soups, stews and casseroles, or prepare it with fish or vegetables for a salad.

 Potatoes: Mash them, boil them, fry them into chips and fries, bake them into wedges, purée them to form the basis of a thick soup, cut into chunks for curries, casseroles and stews, roast them, make them into fishcakes, bubble and squeak, moussaka, shepherd's pie, fish pie, hash browns, potato salad or the standard baked potato.

 Noodles: Use noodles in stir-fries and soups, as ramen-style noodles, egg-fried noodles, or plain noodles to accompany another dish.

 Pasta (shapes, not ravioli, cannelloni, tortellini or spaghetti): Eat pasta freshly cooked and tossed in a sauce or accompanying 'meat and two veg', or make macaroni cheese, macaroni milk pudding, pasta bakes or pasta salad, or put pasta in soups and stews (such as minestrone soup).

Versatile Meat

There is more to meat than a roast dinner or bangers and mash. We will come on to the different fresh meat cuts that you can get to suit every type of budget, but let us look at ways of using variations on the meat theme, taking some of the cheapest available meat products:

 Burger meat: Available in big freezer packs and often at a discount, it is tempting just to slap these between two slices of bread roll with some cheese and bacon. However, they can also be used to make stews, hearty soups, casseroles, patties and pies and pasta sauces (if cooked and broken up with some onion, herbs and chopped tomatoes).

✅ **Minced/ground meat**: This can be used to make various bulk meals that can be stored and frozen for future use. Some of its uses include bubble and squeak, chilli con carne, lasagne, meatloaf, meatballs, pasta sauce, pies and patties, rissoles, shepherd's pie, cottage pie and meat timbales.

✅ **Tinned meat**: This includes tinned ham, spam and that other staple from the Second World War, corned beef. Ways to use these include bubble and squeak, cold sandwiches, cold as part of a ploughman's lunch, hot sandwiches such as melts, shepherd's pie, pastries, rissoles, sliced into salads, in pasta dishes (tinned ham, cut into chunks) and in soups.

✅ **Sandwich (sliced, packaged) meat**: This does not just have to be put into sandwiches. It can also be used in the following ways: in hot melts, added to pizza topping, eaten cold as part of a ploughman's or other light lunch, salads (sliced thinly), mixed into pasta dishes such as carbonara, pastries and croque monsieurs/madames.

✅ **Sausages**: Delightful hot or cold, on their own or inside a roll or sandwich, they can also be used in a sausage and pepper casserole; cooked, sliced and added to beans; diced up in a lasagne; cut up into chunks and added to stews; served cold, sliced, with salad; or in pastries.

Fishy Tales

Whether you get your fish right from the wharf, out of a tin or a cut from the supermarket, you can cook it many ways. Some of these methods can create a big quantity of food for a small amount of money. These dishes can then be put into the freezer to save for another day. Ways to cook or use fish (tinned, frozen or fresh) include: cold inside sandwiches (tinned) or as a filling for baked potatoes; in curries, kedgerees, paellas, fish chowders, roulades, fisherman's pie, pasta bakes, pastries, mousses, kebabs or warm salads; baked, poached, grilled/broiled, fried (with or without batter), mashed with potatoes to make fishcakes, pickled or breadcrumbed; or eaten on their own, accompanied by rice or salad and bread.

Vegetable Delights

It is surprising how many ways vegetables can be used, when they are usually thought of as accompaniments to the meat-and-potatoes section of a meal. You can use vegetables in pasta dishes, curries, lasagnes, kebabs, pies, pastries, rice dishes, stir-fries, casseroles, stews, soups and salads. You can serve them roasted, baked (half an aubergine can be hollowed out, the flesh mixed with tomatoes and onion and the aubergine shell refilled with the mixture, then baked with cheese, for example), stuffed (peppers can be stuffed with rice or meat, for instance), barbecued, grilled within hot melts, made into vegetarian burgers and sausages or, of course, raw.

Cheap Cuts of Meat

One student from Australia claimed that meat is just too expensive to be part of the diet for someone living on a tight budget. But this is not actually the case. What is true is that people used to going to the supermarket to buy their meat will only be presented with the prices on the counter. More than that, they will only be offered meat from a limited selection of cuts and produce. This gives the false impression that meat is too expensive to be able to be part of a 'cheap meal challenge'.

Think Continental

Speaking to a Hungarian gentleman of advanced years, he proclaimed, 'I don't understand why young families these days say they cannot afford meat. We escaped from Hungary with nothing but the clothes on our backs and yet always ate well. But you Anglo-Saxons don't know about cheap cuts of meat.' Well, that is not entirely true. We do, or we did during the war years, but most of us have forgotten what these cuts are. Cheap cuts of meat include:

- cheeks
- trotters
- liver
- hock
- shoulder
- chump
- oxtail
- skirt
- brisket
- tongue (technically offal – see below)

Where Do You Get These?

These are all available at butchers and markets, particularly specialist meat markets. You can also buy some of them from the fresh meat sections of the larger superstores, although the variety will be restricted and you will be paying retail, not wholesale, prices.

How to Cook Cheap Cuts of Meat

The cheap cuts of meat are often less expensive because they tend to be tougher than the usual cuts such as t-bone or rib-eye. But they are also lean (less fatty) and, with the right treatment, are extremely tasty. Some suggestions include:

Cheeks: Beef cheeks are gaining in popularity in top restaurants, particularly as businesspeople are reducing their entertainment budgets and exploring different options. Try slow-cooking beef cheeks in some red wine or a treacle and vinegar sauce for a few hours until tender. Serve hot in its juices with some creamy mash, roast parsnips and hot English mustard.

Oxtail: This is the tail of a steer or cow and is notoriously tough. Tenderise it and slow-cook it in a meaty broth until the juices permeate the liquid. Cut away the meat and boil it up in a stew, together with chunks of carrot, leeks and turnip or swede. Serve on its own or with baby new potatoes.

Skirt: This is the underpart, or belly, of a cow or lamb. This is a very lean meat and can take up to 6 hours until it is tender enough to eat. Tenderise it and put it in a slow-cooker or hay box along with some stock and chopped vegetables. When you get home, add some fresh dumplings and serve.

Tongue: Although technically offal, this is a delicious meat and can be bought very cheaply. It is also versatile, and can be used, when cold, as sandwich filling: add some ciabatta, onion relish and some salad leaves and provide yourself with a top-quality meat sandwich.

Offal

This is basically everything else left over when the main flesh has been taken from the carcass of an animal, such as head, brain, brawn, snout, tongue, tripe, giblets and so on. Dishes using offal were very popular even 40 years ago and were often sold as basic pub grub alongside the traditional steak and chips. However, there are various reasons why offal has lost its popularity, not least because of the meat scares of the 1990s, with CJD (the human variant of BSE) and scrapie, meaning that people shunned meat. Many are only just starting to come back to it but do not feel brave enough to deal with offal.

I Would Never Eat Those!

But you eat sausages, haggis and re-formed meat burgers – what do you think they use to make them? You might like to eat steak and kidney pie or liver as part of a mixed grill. You may have eaten Scrapple sandwiches in the States (using meat made from a combination of pig offal) and maybe munched through some Rocky Mountain Oysters, which are bulls' testes. Moreover, if you have eaten some of these things, you probably really enjoyed them.

A Last Word

There are so many ways to make a cheap meal that can include meat in various forms and fresh fish. You do not have to resort to bargain basement packets of burgers and fish fingers. When thinking about your own family's cheap meal challenge, try going beyond the boundaries of what you have been used to, or the 'easy' options presented by the supermarkets. The more you can cook these dishes, the more varied the menu will become, all the while sticking to your budget – and even cutting your budget further.

Case Study: The Appleyards

Christopher and Rhian Appleyard, from Surrey, and their student children Rachel (21) and Richard (19) tried the taste challenge. They found that they could plan and prepare a two-course meal well within £5 and still have some food – and change – left over. Rhian reports, 'This is a tried-and-tested regular meal: turkey spaghetti Bolognese with fresh tomatoes, and organic fruit yogurt for dessert. I usually keep a portion of the Bolognese for my lunch the next day so it serves five people, not four. I went to a well-known international supermarket chain to buy the ingredients.' The breakdown is:

- turkey mince £1.78
- own-brand mushroom pasta sauce 88p
- own-brand basics range value spaghetti 39p
- organic plum tomatoes 66p
- Biopot wholegrain peach yogurt £1.24

Total £4.95

Store-cupboard Ingredients

It is essential to have a store cupboard full of ingredients that form the basis of many meals, or that you particularly like to use. Many store cupboard ingredients tend to have long shelf lives and to be used in fairly small quantities, so you only need to spend on them now and then. Obviously you can add to them at any time. One word of caution however, do not buy very large bottles, packets or tubs until you know how much you will use them.

What to Buy for the Recipes in this Book

Below is a comprehensive list of 'store-cupboard ingredients' that are featured in the recipes this book – most of these aren't counted as part of the 'up to £5' total as you should not have to buy them each time you make a specific recipe.

 Oil: For cooking, use olive, sunflower, vegetable or groundnut oil. Do not cook with extra virgin olive oil – reserve that for things like salad dressings. Cooking destroys the delicate flavour and aroma of extra virgin olive oil and as it is the most expensive oil it is simply a waste to cook with it.

 Vinegars: When vinegar is called for, white wine vinegar is often a good option, as it will impart a more delicate flavour than a vinegar such as malt or cider, and it is not as expensive as balsamic or rice wine vinegar. It is a very versatile vinegar and can be used in stews and casseroles as well as sauces and marinades as well as Asian-style dishes such as stir fries.

Stock cubes or powders: Beef, fish and vegetable stock cubes are essential (unless you've made your own stock!)

Spices: These are especially useful if spicy food is a firm favourite. Remember to keep them in a cool dark place so as to preserve their pungency and aroma. Useful dried spices are: ground cumin, ground coriander, ground cinnamon, turmeric, paprika, ground ginger, chilli/cayenne powder, salt, black pepper, mixed spices, ground ginger, Chinese five-spice powder and curry powder. You can also buy many of these unground, as seeds, which you grind yourself with a pestle and mortar, for even more flavour. Curry paste, in Korma or Madras varieties for example, also goes a fairly long way. Even saffron is not necessarily out of your league, as, despite being the most expensive spice, you need very little to add a special flavour and colour to dishes. And, properly stored, saffron strands can last for several years. If you prefer, turmeric can always be used in place of saffron in order to impart colour.

Herbs: Dried herbs are much cheaper than fresh (but if you grown your own herbs then great!). Again, store in a cool dark place and buy in small quantities. Good ones to have are oregano, thyme, sage, parsley and mixed herbs.

Plain and self-raising flour: These are essential store cupboard ingredients. Plain flour is used for making pastry (it is so much cheaper to make pastry than buy it), biscuits and cookies, thickening casseroles and stews, savoury sauces and gravies and coating food prior to shallow frying. Self-raising flour ensures perfect cakes and baked puddings, as the ratio of raising agent and flour has already been measured out. This means there is less need to buy separate baking powder or bicarbonate of soda.

Cornflour: This is used to thicken sauces – especially useful if watching calorie intake.

Tomato purée: This is best if bought in a tube then, once opened, stored in the refrigerator to give it the best shelf life.

✔️ **Soy and hoisin sauce**: Either dark or light soy sauce. Dark soy sauce tends to be slightly thicker, sweeter and richer. Hoisin sauce is a ready-made dipping sauce, which includes soy sauce in its ingredients, but it is also used as a cooking ingredient.

✔️ **Other sauces**: There are so many to choose from so only buy them if you think you are going to get a good deal of use out of them. Hot pepper sauce, Tabasco or sweet chilli sauce are some that might be valuable.

✔️ **Clear honey**: Buy in a squeezy bottle as this makes it easier to use.

✔️ **Sugar**: This is useful for many recipes and having a selection is worthwhile, especially if you bake. Ideal sugars to stock would be granulated, caster, soft brown and icing sugar.

Store-cupboard Items You Will Need To Buy More Often

✔️ **Canned tomatoes**: Probably one of the most frequently used canned items. Whole tomatoes in cans are cheaper to buy then the chopped variety.

✔️ **Canned beans**: Mixed, kidney, cannellini and chickpeas are commonly used beans.

✔️ **Pasta**: You'll get through a lot of this but it is cheap and stores well. Two good staples to have are penne and spaghetti.

✔️ **Rice**: Similar staple to pasta. Main types to have are long-grain or basmati, both white and brown, and risotto rice.

✔️ **Other grains**: Couscous and lentils are also versatile and handy to have to hand.

Recipes: Soups & Starters

Italian Bean Soup

Ingredients (Serves 4)

2 tsp olive oil
1 leek, washed and chopped
1 garlic clove, peeled and crushed
2 tsp dried oregano
75 g/3 oz green beans, trimmed and cut into
  bite-size pieces
410 g can cannellini beans, drained and rinsed
75 g/3 oz small pasta shapes
1 litre/1¾ pint vegetable stock
8 cherry tomatoes
salt and freshly ground black pepper
3 tbsp freshly shredded basil (optional)

Heat the oil in a large saucepan.
Add the leek, garlic and oregano and
cook gently for 5 minutes, stirring
occasionally.

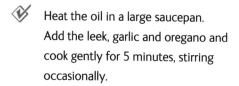

Stir in the green beans and the
cannellini beans. Sprinkle in the pasta
and pour in the stock.

Bring the stock mixture to the boil,
then reduce the heat to a simmer.

Cook for 12–15 minutes until the
vegetables are tender and the pasta is
cooked to *al dente*. Stir occasionally.

In a heavy-based frying pan, dry-fry
the tomatoes over a high heat
until they soften and the skins begin
to blacken.

✔ Gently crush the tomatoes in the pan with the back of a spoon and add to the soup.

✔ Season to taste with salt and pepper. Stir in the shredded basil, if using, and serve immediately.

Tasty Tip

1 teaspoon dried herbs equals
1 tablespoon fresh herbs.

Rich Tomato Soup with Roasted Red Pepper

Ingredients (Serves 4)

2 tbsp olive oil
4 red peppers, halved and deseeded
450 g/1 lb ripe plum tomatoes, halved
2 onions, unpeeled and quartered
4 garlic cloves, unpeeled
600 ml/1 pint chicken or vegetable stock
salt and freshly ground black pepper
4 tbsp soured cream
1 tbsp freshly shredded basil

 Preheat oven to 200°C/400°F/Gas Mark 6. Lightly oil a roasting tin with 1 teaspoon of the olive oil. Place the peppers and tomatoes cut side down in the roasting tin with the onion quarters and the garlic cloves. Spoon over the remaining oil.

 Bake in the preheated oven for 30 minutes, or until the skins on the peppers have started to blacken and blister. Allow the vegetables to cool for about 10 minutes, then remove the skins, stalks and seeds from the peppers. Peel away the skins from the tomatoes and onions and squeeze out the garlic.

 Place the cooked vegetables into a blender or food processor and blend until smooth. Add the stock and blend again to form a smooth purée. Pour the puréed soup through a sieve, if a smooth soup is preferred, then pour into a saucepan. Bring to the boil, simmer gently for 2–3 minutes, and season to taste with salt and pepper. Serve hot with a swirl of soured cream and a sprinkling of shredded basil on the top.

Helpful Hint
To help remove the skins of the peppers more easily, remove them from the oven and put immediately into a plastic bag or a bowl covered with clingfilm. Leave until cool enough to handle then skin carefully.

Pumpkin and Smoked Haddock Soup

Ingredients (Serves 4)

2 tbsp olive or sunflower oil
1 medium onion, peeled and chopped
2 garlic cloves, peeled and chopped
1 celery stalk, trimmed and chopped
450 g/1 lb pumpkin, peeled, deseeded and cut
  into chunks
450 g/1 lb potatoes, peeled and cut into chunks
900 ml/1½ pints fish or chicken stock, heated
175 g/6 oz smoked haddock fillet
150 ml/¼ pint milk
freshly ground black pepper
2 tbsp freshly chopped parsley

Heat the oil in a large heavy-based saucepan and gently cook the onion, garlic and celery for about 10 minutes. This will release the sweetness but not colour the vegetables. Add the pumpkin and potatoes to the saucepan and stir to coat the vegetables with the oil.

Gradually pour in the stock and bring to the boil. Cover, then reduce the heat and simmer for 25 minutes, stirring occasionally. Remove the saucepan from the heat and leave to cool for 5–10 minutes.

Blend the mixture in a food processor or blender to form a chunky purée and return to the cleaned saucepan.

Meanwhile, place the fish in a shallow frying pan. Pour in the milk with 3 tablespoons of water and bring to almost boiling point. Reduce the heat, cover and simmer for 6 minutes, or until the fish is cooked and flakes easily. Remove from the heat and, using a slotted spoon, remove the fish from the liquid, reserving both liquid and fish.

Discard the skin and any bones from the fish and flake into pieces. Stir the fish liquid into the soup, together with the flaked fish. Season with freshly ground black pepper, stir in the parsley and serve immediately.

Helpful Hint
Try to find undyed smoked haddock for this soup rather than the brightly coloured yellow type, as the texture and flavour are better.

Bacon and Split Pea Soup

Ingredients (Serves 4)

50 g/2 oz dried split peas
25 g/1 oz margarine or butter
1 garlic clove, peeled and finely chopped
1 medium onion, peeled and thinly sliced
125 g/4 oz long-grain rice
2 tbsp tomato purée
1.1 litres/2 pints vegetable or chicken stock
175 g/ 6 oz carrots, peeled and finely diced
125 g/4 oz streaky bacon, finely chopped
salt and freshly ground black pepper
2 tbsp freshly chopped parsley
4 tbsp single cream
warm crusty garlic bread, to serve

Melt the margarine or butter in a heavy-based saucepan, add the garlic and onion and cook for 2–3 minutes, without colouring. Add the rice, drained split peas and tomato purée and cook for 2–3 minutes, stirring constantly to prevent sticking. Add the stock, bring to the boil, then reduce the heat and simmer for 20–25 minutes until the rice and peas are tender. Remove from the heat and leave to cool.

Cover the dried split peas with plenty of cold water, cover loosely and leave to soak for a minimum of 12 hours, preferably overnight.

Blend about three quarters of the soup in a food processor or blender to form a smooth purée. Pour the purée into the remaining soup in the

saucepan. Add the carrots to the saucepan and cook for a further 10–12 minutes until the carrots are tender.

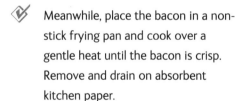 Meanwhile, place the bacon in a non-stick frying pan and cook over a gentle heat until the bacon is crisp. Remove and drain on absorbent kitchen paper.

Season the soup with salt and pepper to taste, then stir in the parsley and cream. Reheat for 2–3 minutes, then ladle into soup bowls. Sprinkle with the bacon and serve immediately with warm garlic bread.

Classic Minestrone

Ingredients (Serves 4-6)

25 g/1 oz margarine or butter
1 tbsp olive oil
2 rashers streaky bacon
1 onion, peeled
1 garlic clove, peeled
1 celery stalk, trimmed
2 carrots, peeled
400 g can whole peeled tomatoes, chopped
1.1 litre/2 pints vegetable or chicken stock
125 g/4 oz green cabbage, finely shredded
50 g/2 oz French beans, trimmed and halved
3 tbsp frozen petits pois
50 g/2 oz spaghetti, broken into short pieces
salt and freshly ground black pepper
Parmesan cheese shavings, to garnish
crusty bread, to serve

Heat the margarine or butter and olive oil together in a large saucepan. Chop the bacon and add to the saucepan. Cook for 3–4 minutes, then remove with a slotted spoon and reserve.

Finely chop the onion, garlic, celery and carrots and add to the saucepan, one ingredient at a time, stirring well after each addition. Cover and cook gently for 8–10 minutes until the vegetables are softened.

Add the chopped tomatoes, with their juice and the stock, bring to the boil then cover the saucepan with a lid, reduce the heat and simmer gently for about 20 minutes.

Stir in the cabbage, beans, peas and spaghetti pieces. Cover and simmer for a further 20 minutes, or until all the ingredients are tender. Season to taste with salt and pepper.

Return the cooked bacon to the saucepan and bring the soup to the boil. Serve the soup immediately with Parmesan cheese shavings sprinkled on the top and plenty of crusty bread to accompany it.

Tasty Tip

There are many different variations of minestrone. You can add drained canned cannellini beans either in place of or as well as the spaghetti, or use small soup pasta shells. For a vegetarian version, omit the bacon and use vegetable stock and a vegetarian cheese.

Cream of Pumpkin Soup

Ingredients (Serves 4)

675 g/1½ lb pumpkin flesh (after peeling and discarding the seeds)
2 tbsp olive oil
1 onion, peeled
1 leek, trimmed
1 carrot, peeled
2 celery sticks
4 garlic cloves, peeled and crushed
1.7 litres/3 pints water
salt and freshly ground black pepper
¼ tsp freshly grated nutmeg
150 ml/¼ pint single cream
¼ tsp cayenne pepper
warm herby bread, to serve

 Cut the skinned and deseeded pumpkin flesh into 2.5 cm/1 inch cubes. Heat the olive oil in a large saucepan and cook the pumpkin for 2–3 minutes, coating it completely with oil. Chop the onion and leek finely and cut the carrot and celery in to small dice.

 Add the vegetables to the saucepan with the garlic and cook, stirring, for 5 minutes, or until they have begun to soften. Cover the vegetables with the water and bring to the boil. Season with plenty of salt and pepper and the nutmeg, cover and simmer for 15–20 minutes until all of the vegetables are tender.

Tasty Tip

If you cannot find pumpkin, try replacing it with squash. Butternut, acorn or turban squash would all make suitable substitutes. Avoid spaghetti squash which is not firm-fleshed when cooked.

 When the vegetables are tender, remove from the heat, cool slightly then pour into a food processor or blender. Liquidise to form a smooth purée then pass through a sieve into a clean saucepan.

 Adjust the seasoning to taste and add all but 2 tablespoons of the cream and enough water to obtain the correct consistency. Bring the soup to boiling point, add the cayenne pepper and serve immediately swirled with the remaining cream and warm herby bread.

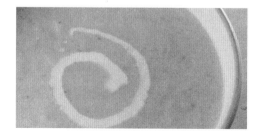

Mozzarella Frittata with Tomato and Basil Salad

Ingredients (Serves 4)

FOR THE SALAD:
4 ripe but firm tomatoes
1 tbsp fresh basil leaves
2 tbsp olive oil
1 tbsp fresh lemon juice
1 tsp caster sugar
freshly ground black pepper

FOR THE FRITTATA:
5 medium eggs, beaten
salt
200 g/7 oz mozzarella cheese
2 spring onions, trimmed and finely chopped
1 tbsp olive oil
warm crusty bread, to serve

 To make the tomato and basil salad, slice the tomatoes very thinly, tear up the basil leaves and sprinkle over. Make the dressing by whisking the olive oil, lemon juice and sugar together well. Season with black pepper before drizzling the dressing over the salad.

 To make the frittata, preheat the grill to a high heat, just before beginning to cook. Place the eggs in a large bowl with salt and whisk. Grate the mozzarella and stir into the egg with the finely chopped spring onions.

 Heat the oil in a large, non-stick frying pan and pour in the egg mixture, stirring with a wooden spoon to spread the ingredients evenly over the pan.

 Cook on the hob for 5–8 minutes until the frittata is golden brown and firm on the underside. Place the whole pan under the preheated grill and cook for about 4–5 minutes until the top is golden brown. Slide the frittata on to a serving plate, cut into four large wedges and serve immediately with the tomato and basil salad and plenty of warm crusty bread.

Helpful Hint

Fresh mozzarella is sold in packets and is usually surrounded by a light brine. After grating the cheese, firmly press between layers of absorbent kitchen paper to remove any excess water which might leak out during cooking.

Bruschetta with Pecorino, Garlic and Tomatoes

Ingredients (Serves 4)

6 ripe but firm tomatoes
125 g/4 oz pecorino cheese, finely grated
1 tbsp oregano leaves
salt and freshly ground black pepper
1 tbsp olive oil
3 garlic cloves, peeled
8 slices flat Italian bread, such as focaccia
50 g/2 oz mozzarella cheese, sliced
marinated black olives, to serve

2 minutes, then drain and remove the skins. Cut into quarters, remove the seeds and chop the flesh into small dice.

Mix the tomato flesh with the pecorino cheese and 2 teaspoons of the fresh oregano and season to taste with salt and pepper. Add 1 tablespoon of the olive oil and mix thoroughly.

Preheat the grill and line the grill rack with foil just before cooking. Make a small cross in the top of the tomatoes, then place in a small bowl and cover with boiling water. Leave to stand for

Crush the garlic and spread evenly over the slices of bread. Heat 2 tablespoons of the olive oil in a large frying pan and fry the bread slices until they are crisp and golden.

Place the fried bread on a lightly oiled baking tray and spoon on the tomato and cheese topping. Place a little mozzarella on top and place under the preheated grill for 3–4 minutes until golden and bubbling. Garnish with the remaining oregano, then arrange the bruschettas on a serving plate and serve immediately with the olives.

Peperonata (Braised Mixed Peppers)

Ingredients (Serves 4)

1 green pepper
1 red pepper
1 yellow pepper
1 orange pepper
1 onion, peeled
2 garlic cloves, peeled
4 very ripe tomatoes
2 tbsp olive oil
1 tbsp freshly chopped oregano
salt and freshly ground black pepper
150 ml/¼ pint chicken or vegetable stock
fresh oregano sprigs, to garnish
focaccia or flat bread, to serve

Remove the seeds from the peppers and cut into thin strips. Slice the onion into rings and chop the garlic cloves finely.

Make a cross on the top of the tomatoes then place in a bowl and cover with boiling water. Allow to

stand for about 2 minutes. Drain, then remove the skins and seeds and chop the tomato flesh into cubes.

Heat the olive oil in a frying pan and fry the peppers, onions and garlic for 5–10 minutes until soft and lightly coloured. Stir continuously.

Add the tomatoes and oregano to the peppers and onion and season to taste with salt and pepper. Cover the pan and bring to the boil. Simmer gently for about 30 minutes until tender, adding the chicken or vegetable stock halfway through the cooking time.

Garnish with sprigs of oregano and serve hot with plenty of freshly baked focaccia bread. Alternatively, lightly toast slices of flat bread and pile a spoonful of peperonata on to each plate.

Tasty Tip
Look for bags of mixed peppers in your local store as they are far cheaper than buying them separately.

Mozzarella Parcels with Cranberry Relish

Ingredients (Serves 4)

75 g/3 oz mozzarella cheese
8 slices thin white bread
2 medium eggs, beaten
salt and freshly ground black pepper
oil for deep frying, preferably olive oil

FOR THE RELISH:
125 g/4 oz cranberries, thawed if frozen
2 tbsp fresh orange juice
grated zest of 1 small orange
50 g/2 oz soft light brown sugar
1 tbsp port, or use extra orange juice

Slice the mozzarella thinly, remove the crusts from the bread and make sandwiches with the bread and cheese. Cut into 5 cm/2 inch squares and squash them quite flat. Season the eggs with salt and pepper, then soak the bread in the seasoned egg for 1 minute on each side until well coated.

Heat the oil to 190°C/375°F and deep-fry the bread squares for 1–2 minutes until they are crisp and golden brown. Drain on absorbent kitchen paper and keep warm while the cranberry relish is prepared.

Place the cranberries, orange juice, zest, sugar and port, if using, into a small saucepan and add 5 tablespoons of water. Bring to the boil, then simmer for 10 minutes, or until the cranberries have 'popped'. Sweeten with a little more sugar if necessary.

Arrange the mozzarella parcels on individual serving plates. Serve with a little of the cranberry relish.

Helpful Hint

Frying in oil that is not hot enough causes food to absorb more oil than it would if fried at the correct temperature. To test the temperature of the oil without a thermometer, drop a cube of bread into the frying pan. If the bread browns in 30 seconds, the oil is at the right temperature.

Pasta with Walnut Sauce

Ingredients (Serves 4)

40 g/1½ oz shelled walnuts, toasted
3 spring onions, trimmed and chopped
2 garlic cloves, peeled and sliced
1 tbsp freshly chopped parsley or basil
3 tbsp olive oil
salt and freshly ground black pepper
225 g/ 8 oz broccoli, cut into florets
175 g/6 oz pasta shapes
1 red chilli, deseeded and finely chopped

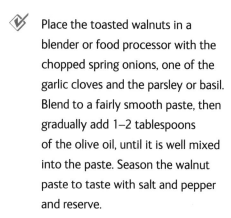

Place the toasted walnuts in a blender or food processor with the chopped spring onions, one of the garlic cloves and the parsley or basil. Blend to a fairly smooth paste, then gradually add 1–2 tablespoons of the olive oil, until it is well mixed into the paste. Season the walnut paste to taste with salt and pepper and reserve.

Bring a large pan of lightly salted water to a rolling boil. Add the broccoli, return to the boil and cook for 2 minutes. Remove the broccoli, using a slotted draining spoon, and refresh under cold running water. Drain again and pat dry on absorbent kitchen paper.

Bring the water back to a rolling boil. Add the pasta and cook according to the packet instructions, or until *al dente*.

Meanwhile, heat the remaining oil in a frying pan. Add the remaining garlic and chilli. Cook gently for 2 minutes, or until softened. Add the broccoli and walnut paste. Cook for a further 3–4 minutes until heated through.

Drain the pasta thoroughly and transfer to a large warmed serving bowl. Pour over the walnut and broccoli sauce. Toss together, adjust the seasoning and serve immediately.

Helpful Hint
This starter will also make a good reasonably priced main meal. Simply double up the ingredients. There is also no hard-and-fast rule about which shape of pasta to use with this recipe; it is really a matter of personal preference.

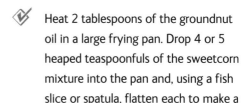

Sweetcorn Fritters

Ingredients (Serves 4)

4 tbsp groundnut oil
1 small onion, peeled and finely chopped
1 red chilli, deseeded and finely chopped
1 garlic clove, peeled and crushed
1 tsp ground coriander
325 g can sweetcorn
6 spring onions, trimmed and finely sliced
1 medium egg, lightly beaten
salt and freshly ground black pepper
3 tbsp plain flour
1 tsp baking powder
spring onion curls, to garnish
Thai-style chutney, to serve

 Heat 1 tablespoon of the groundnut oil in a frying pan, add the onion and cook gently for 7–8 minutes until beginning to soften. Add the chilli, garlic and ground coriander and cook for 1 minute, stirring continuously. Remove from the heat.

 Drain the sweetcorn and tip into a mixing bowl. Lightly mash with a potato masher to break down the corn a little. Add the cooked onion mixture to the bowl with the spring onions and beaten egg. Season to taste with salt and pepper, then stir to mix together. Sift the flour and baking powder over the mixture and stir in.

 Heat 2 tablespoons of the groundnut oil in a large frying pan. Drop 4 or 5 heaped teaspoonfuls of the sweetcorn mixture into the pan and, using a fish slice or spatula, flatten each to make a 1 cm/$\frac{1}{2}$ inch-thick fritter.

Fry the fritters for 3 minutes, or until golden brown on the underside, turn over and fry for a further 3 minutes, or until cooked through and crisp.

Remove the fritters from the pan and drain on absorbent kitchen paper. Keep warm while cooking the remaining fritters, adding a little more oil if needed. Garnish with spring onion curls and serve immediately with a Thai-style chutney.

Hot and Sour Squid

Ingredients (Serves 4)

8 baby squid, cleaned
2 tbsp dark soy sauce
2 tbsp hoisin sauce
1 tbsp lime juice
2 tbsp dry sherry
1 tbsp clear honey
2.5 cm/1 inch piece fresh root ginger, peeled and
    finely chopped
1 red chilli, deseeded and finely chopped
1 green chilli, deseeded and finely chopped
1 tsp cornflour
salt and freshly ground black pepper
vegetable oil for deep-frying
lime wedges, to garnish

 Slice open the body of each squid lengthways, open out and place on a chopping board with the inside uppermost. Using a sharp knife, score lightly in a criss-cross pattern. Cut each one into four pieces. Trim the tentacles.

 Place the soy and hoisin sauces with the lime juice, sherry, honey, ginger, chillies and cornflour in a bowl. Season to taste with salt and pepper and mix together. Add the squid, stir well to coat, then cover and place in the refrigerator to marinate for 1 hour.

Tip the squid into a sieve over a small saucepan and strain off the marinade. Scrape any bits of chilli or ginger into the saucepan, as they would burn if fried.

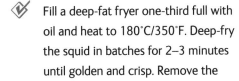

Fill a deep-fat fryer one-third full with oil and heat to 180°C/350°F. Deep-fry the squid in batches for 2–3 minutes until golden and crisp. Remove the squid and drain on absorbent kitchen paper. Keep warm.

Bring the marinade to the boil and let it bubble gently for a few seconds. Arrange the squid on a warmed serving dish and drizzle over the marinade. Garnish with lime wedges and serve immediately.

Helpful Hint

It is simple to prepare squid. Rinse well in cold water, then firmly pull apart the head and body; the innards will come away with the head. Remove and discard the transparent beak. Rinse the body pouch thoroughly under cold running water and peel off the thin layer of dark skin. The tentacles are edible, so cut them away from the head just below the eyes. They can also be deep-fried to be used in this dish, if liked.

Smoked Mackerel Vol-au-Vents

Ingredients (Makes 4)

350 g/12 oz ready-made puff pastry
1 small egg, beaten
2 tsp sesame seeds
225 g/8 oz peppered smoked mackerel,
    skinned and chopped
5 cm/2 inch piece cucumber
4 tbsp soft cream cheese
2 tbsp cranberry sauce
1 tbsp freshly chopped dill
1 tbsp finely grated lemon zest
dill sprigs, to garnish
mixed salad leaves, to serve

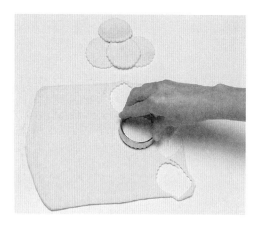

Preheat the oven to 230°C/450°F/Gas Mark 8. Roll the pastry out on a lightly floured surface and, using a 9 cm/3½ inch fluted cutter, cut out eight rounds.

Using a 1 cm/½ inch cutter, mark a lid in the centre of four of the rounds.

Place the plain rounds on a damp baking sheet and brush them with a little beaten egg. Place the remaining rounds (with marked lids) on top and press the edges lightly together.

Sprinkle the pastry with the sesame seeds and bake in the preheated oven for 10–12 minutes until golden brown and well risen.

Transfer the vol-au-vents to a chopping board and, when cool enough to touch, carefully remove the lids with a small sharp knife.

Scoop out any uncooked pastry from the inside of each vol-au-vent, then return to the oven for 5–8 minutes to dry out. Remove and allow to cool.

 Beat the soft cream cheese with the cranberry sauce, chopped dill and lemon zest. Stir in the mackerel and cucumber and use to fill the vol-au-vents. Place the lids on top and garnish with dill sprigs.

Food Fact

Mackerel is a relatively cheap fish and one of the richest sources of minerals, oils and vitamins available. This dish is an affordable way to incorporate all these essential nutrients into your diet

Flake the mackerel into small pieces and reserve. Peel the cucumber if desired, cut into very small dice and add to the mackerel.

Fennel and Caramelised Shallot Tartlets

Ingredients (Serves 6)

FOR THE CHEESE PASTRY:
175 g/6 oz plain white flour
75 g/3 oz margarine or slightly salted butter
50 g/2 oz Gruyère cheese, grated
1 small egg yolk

FOR THE FILLING:
2 tbsp olive oil
225 g/8 oz shallots, peeled and halved
1 fennel bulb, trimmed and sliced
1 tsp soft brown sugar
1 medium egg
150 ml/¼ pint single cream
salt and freshly ground black pepper
25 g/1 oz Gruyère cheese, grated
½ tsp ground cinnamon
mixed salad leaves, to serve

Preheat the oven to 200°C/400°F/Gas Mark 6. To make the pastry, sift the flour into a bowl, then rub in the margarine or butter, using the fingertips. Stir in the cheese, then add the egg yolk with about 2 tablespoons of cold water. Mix to a firm dough, then knead lightly. Wrap in clingfilm and chill in the refrigerator for 30 minutes.

Roll out the pastry on a lightly floured surface and use to line six 10 cm/4 inch round individual flan tins or patty tins that are about 2 cm/³⁄₄ inch deep.

Line the pastry cases with greaseproof paper and fill with baking beans or rice. Bake blind in the preheated oven for about 10 minutes, then remove the paper and beans.

Heat the oil in a frying pan, add the shallots and fennel and fry gently for 5 minutes. Sprinkle with the sugar and cook for a further 10 minutes, stirring occasionally, until lightly caramelised. Reserve until cooled.

Beat together the egg and cream and season to taste with salt and pepper. Divide the shallot mixture between the pastry cases. Pour over the egg mixture and sprinkle with the cheese and cinnamon. Bake for 20 minutes, or until golden and set. Serve with the salad leaves.

Olive and Feta Parcels

Ingredients (Makes 30)

1 small red pepper
1 small yellow pepper
125 g/4 oz assorted marinated green and black olives
125 g/4 oz feta cheese
2 tbsp pine nuts, lightly toasted
6 sheets filo pastry
3 tbsp olive oil
sour cream and chive dip, to serve

Preheat the oven to 180°C/350°F/Gas Mark 4. Preheat the grill, then line the grill rack with foil.

Cut the peppers into quarters and remove the seeds. Place skin side up on the foil-lined grill rack and cook under the preheated grill for 10 minutes, turning occasionally, until the skins begin to blacken.

Place the peppers in a polythene bag and leave until cool enough to handle, then skin and thinly slice.

Chop the olives and cut the feta cheese into small cubes. Mix together the olives, feta, sliced peppers and pine nuts.

Cut 1 sheet of filo pastry in half then brush with a little of the oil. Place a spoonful of the olive and feta mix one third of the way up the pastry.

Fold over the pastry and wrap to form a square parcel encasing the filling completely.

Place this parcel in the centre of the second half of the pastry sheet. Brush the edges lightly with a little oil, bring up the corners to meet in the centre and twist them loosely to form a purse.

Brush with a little more oil and repeat with the remaining filo pastry and filling.

Place the parcels on a lightly oiled baking sheet and bake in the preheated oven for 10–15 minutes until crisp and golden brown. Serve with the dip.

Recipes: Fish & Seafood

Smoked Haddock Tart

Ingredients (Serves 6)

FOR THE SHORTCRUST PASTRY:
150 g/5 oz plain flour
pinch salt
25 g/1 oz white vegetable fat, cut into small cubes
40 g/1½ oz butter or hard margarine, cut into small cubes

FOR THE FILLING:
225 g/8 oz smoked haddock, skinned and cubed
2 large eggs, beaten
300 ml/½ pint single cream
1 tsp Dijon mustard
freshly ground black pepper
125 g/4 oz Gruyère cheese, grated
1 tbsp freshly snipped chives

TO SERVE:
lemon wedges
tomato wedges
fresh green salad leaves

Preheat the oven to 190°C/375°F/Gas Mark 5. To make the pastry, sift the flour and salt into a large bowl. Add the fats and mix lightly. Using the fingertips, rub into the flour until the mixture resembles breadcrumbs.

Sprinkle 1 tablespoon of cold water into the mixture and, with a knife, start bringing the dough together. (It may be necessary to use the hands for the final stage.) If the dough does not form a ball instantly, add a little more water.

Put the pastry in a polythene bag and chill for at least 30 minutes.

On a lightly floured surface, roll out the pastry and use to line a 18 cm/7 inch lightly oiled quiche or flan tin. Prick the base all over with a fork and bake blind in the preheated oven for 15 minutes.

Carefully remove the pastry from the oven and brush with a little of the beaten egg.

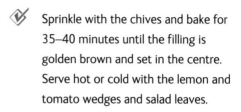

Return to the oven for a further 5 minutes, then place the fish in the pastry case.

For the filling, beat together the eggs and cream. Add the mustard, black pepper and cheese and pour over the fish.

Sprinkle with the chives and bake for 35–40 minutes until the filling is golden brown and set in the centre. Serve hot or cold with the lemon and tomato wedges and salad leaves.

Food Fact

Haddock is a good low-fat source of protein as well as containing vitamins B6 and B12 and niacin.

Luxury Fish Pasties

Ingredients (Serves 4)

75 g/3 oz margarine or butter
75 g/3 oz plain flour
250 ml/8 fl oz milk
175 g/6 oz salmon fillet, skinned and cut into
    small pieces
1 tbsp freshly chopped parsley
1 tbsp freshly chopped dill
grated zest and juice of 1 lime
75 g/3 oz peeled prawns, thawed if frozen
salt and freshly ground black pepper
350 g/12 oz ready-made puff pastry
1 small egg, beaten
1 tsp sea salt
fresh green salad leaves, to serve

Preheat the oven to 200°C/400°F/Gas Mark 6. Place the margarine or butter in a saucepan and slowly heat until melted.

Add the flour and cook, stirring, for 1 minute. Remove from the heat and gradually add the milk a little at a time, stirring between each addition.

Return to the heat and simmer, stirring continuously until thickened. Remove from the heat and add the salmon, parsley, dill, lime zest, lime juice, prawns and seasoning.

Roll out the pastry on a lightly floured surface and cut out 4 x 12.5 cm/5 inch circles and 4 x 15 cm/6 inch circles.

Brush the edges of the smaller circles with the beaten egg and place two tablespoons of filling in the centre of each one.

Place the larger circles over the filling and press the edges together to seal.

Pinch the edge of the pastry between the forefinger and thumb to ensure a firm seal and decorative edge.

Cut a slit in each parcel, brush with the beaten egg and sprinkle with sea salt.

Transfer to a baking sheet and cook in the preheated oven for 20 minutes, or until golden brown. Serve immediately with some fresh green salad leaves.

Fish Puff Tart

Ingredients (Serves 4)

350 g/12 oz ready-made puff pastry, thawed if frozen
150 g/5 oz smoked haddock
150 g/5 oz pollack or whiting
1 tbsp pesto
2 tomatoes, sliced
125 g/4 oz goats' cheese, sliced
1 medium egg, beaten
freshly chopped parsley, to garnish

Preheat the oven to 220°C/425°F/Gas Mark 7. On a lightly floured surface, roll out the pastry into a 20 x 25 cm/ 8 x 10 inch rectangle.

Draw a 18 x 23 cm/7 x 9 inch rectangle in the centre of the pastry, to form a 2.5 cm/1 inch border. (Be careful not to cut through the pastry.)

Lightly cut criss-cross patterns in the border of the pastry with a knife.

Place the fish on a chopping board and skin with a sharp knife. Cut into thin slices.

Spread the pesto evenly over the bottom of the pastry case with the back of a spoon.

Arrange the fish, tomatoes and cheese in the pastry case and brush the pastry with the beaten egg.

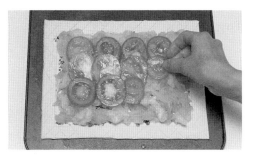

Bake the tart in the preheated oven for 20–25 minutes until the pastry is well risen, puffed and golden brown. Garnish with the chopped parsley and serve immediately.

Helpful Hint
After opening the jar of pesto, screw the lid down tightly and store in the refrigerator for up to 4 weeks.

Mussels with Creamy Garlic and Saffron Sauce

Ingredients (Serves 4)

700 g/1½ lb fresh live mussels
300 ml/½ pint dry white wine and water, mixed
1 tbsp olive oil
1 shallot, peeled and finely chopped
2 garlic cloves, peeled and crushed
1 tbsp freshly chopped oregano
2 saffron strands
150 ml/¼ pint single cream
salt and freshly ground black pepper
fresh crusty bread, to serve

Clean the mussels thoroughly in plenty of cold water and remove any beards and barnacles from the shells. Discard any mussels that are open or damaged. Place in a large bowl and cover with cold water and place a large plate on top. Leave in the refrigerator until required.

Pour the wine and water into a large saucepan and bring to the boil. Tip the mussels into the pan, cover and cook, shaking the saucepan periodically, for 6–8 minutes until the mussels have opened completely.

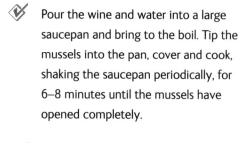

Using a slotted spoon, carefully remove the open mussels; discard any mussels that are closed. Keep the mussels warm. Reserve the cooking liquor.

Heat the olive oil in a small frying pan and cook the shallot and garlic gently for 2–3 minutes until softened. Add the reserved cooking liquor and chopped oregano and cook for a further 3–4 minutes. Stir in the saffron and the cream and heat through gently. Season to taste with salt and pepper. Place the mussels in individual serving bowls and spoon over the saffron sauce. Serve immediately with plenty of fresh crusty bread.

Helpful Hint

Mussels are now farmed and are available most of the year. However, always try to buy mussels the day you intend to eat them. Place them in a bowl of cold water and leave in the refrigerator as soon as possible, changing the water at least every 2 hours.

Marinated Mackerel with Tomato and Basil Salad

Ingredients (Serves 4)

4 mackerel, filleted
4 beefsteak tomatoes, sliced
75 g/3 oz watercress
2 oranges, peeled and segmented
75 g/3 oz mozzarella cheese, sliced
2 tbsp basil leaves, shredded
fresh basil sprig, to garnish

FOR THE MARINADE:
juice of 1 lemon
3 tbsp olive oil
2 tbsp basil leaves

FOR THE DRESSING:
1 tbsp lemon juice
1 tsp Dijon mustard
1 tsp caster sugar
salt and freshly ground black pepper
3 tbsp olive oil

Remove as many of the fine pin bones as possible from the mackerel fillets, lightly rinse and pat dry with absorbent kitchen paper and place in a shallow dish.

Blend the marinade ingredients together and pour over the mackerel fillets. Make sure the marinade has covered the fish completely. Cover and leave in a cool place for at least 8 hours, but preferably overnight. As the fillets marinate, they will lose the translucency and look as if they are cooked.

Place the tomatoes, watercress, oranges and mozzarella cheese in a large bowl and toss.

To make the dressing, whisk the lemon juice with the mustard, sugar, seasoning and oil in a bowl. Pour over half the dressing, toss again and then arrange on a serving platter. Remove the mackerel from the marinade, cut into bite-sized pieces and sprinkle with the shredded basil. Arrange on top of the salad, drizzle over the remaining dressing, scatter with basil leaves and garnish with a basil sprig. Serve.

Food Fact

This dish is based on ceviche, which is a dish of thinly sliced raw fish marinated in lemon juice with other flavourings. Make sure that the fish is absolutely fresh for this dish – use a busy fishmonger, who will have a high turnover and therefore a fresh supply.

Mussels Linguine

Ingredients (Serves 4)

700 g/1½ lb fresh mussels, washed and scrubbed
knob butter
1 onion, peeled and finely chopped
300 ml/½ pint medium dry white wine and
   water, mixed

FOR THE SAUCE:
1 tbsp sunflower oil
4 baby onions, peeled and quartered
2 garlic cloves, peeled and crushed
400 g can whole peeled tomatoes, chopped
large pinch salt
225 g/8 oz dried linguine or tagliatelle
2 tbsp freshly chopped parsley

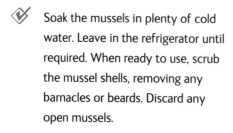 Soak the mussels in plenty of cold water. Leave in the refrigerator until required. When ready to use, scrub the mussel shells, removing any barnacles or beards. Discard any open mussels.

Melt the butter in a large pan. Add the mussels, onion and wine. Cover with a close-fitting lid and steam for 5–6 minutes, shaking the pan gently to ensure even cooking. Discard any mussels that have not opened, then strain and reserve the liquor.

To make the sauce, heat the oil in a medium-sized saucepan, and gently fry the quartered onions and garlic for

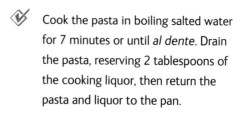

3–4 minutes until soft and transparent. Stir in the tomatoes and half the reserved mussel liquor. Bring to the boil and simmer for 7–10 minutes until the sauce begins to thicken.

Cook the pasta in boiling salted water for 7 minutes or until *al dente*. Drain the pasta, reserving 2 tablespoons of the cooking liquor, then return the pasta and liquor to the pan.

Remove the meat from half the mussel shells. Stir into the sauce along with the remaining mussels. Pour the hot sauce over the cooked pasta and toss gently. Garnish with the parsley and serve immediately.

Helpful Hint

Cans of whole peeled tomatoes are far cheaper than cans of chopped tomatoes. Look for supermarkets' own-label cans.

Smoked Haddock Kedgeree

Ingredients (Serves 4)

300 g/10 oz smoked haddock fillets
50 g/2 oz margarine or butter
1 onion, peeled and finely chopped
2 tsp mild curry powder
175 g/6 oz long-grain rice
450 ml/³/₄ pint fish or vegetable stock, heated
2 large eggs, hard-boiled and shelled
2 tbsp freshly chopped parsley
salt and freshly ground black pepper
pinch cayenne pepper

Place the haddock in a shallow frying pan and cover with 300 ml/¹/₂ pint water. Simmer gently for 8–10 minutes until the fish is cooked. Drain, then remove all the skin and bones from the fish and flake into a dish. Keep warm.

Melt the margarine or butter in a saucepan and add the chopped onion and curry powder. Cook, stirring, for 3–4 minutes until the onion is soft, then stir in the rice. Cook for a further minute, stirring continuously, then stir in the hot stock.

Cover and simmer gently for 15 minutes, or until the rice has absorbed all the liquid. Cut the eggs into quarters and add half to the mixture with half the parsley.

Carefully fold in the cooked fish to the mixture. Season to taste with salt and pepper. Heat the kedgeree through until piping hot.

Transfer the mixture to a large dish and garnish with the remaining quartered eggs and parsley and serve sprinkled with cayenne pepper. Serve immediately.

Food Fact

The word *khichri* means a mixture or hotchpotch in Hindi. The British in India adapted this dish, which was originally made with an assortment of spices simmered with rice and lentils, and turned it into kedgeree, adding flakes of smoked fish and hard-boiled eggs.

Russian Fish Pie

Ingredients (Serves 4)

350 g/12 oz pollack or whiting fillet
150 ml/¼ pint fish stock
salt and freshly ground black pepper
50 g/2 oz margarine or butter
1 onion, peeled and finely chopped
50 g/2 oz long-grain rice
1 tbsp freshly chopped dill
50 g/2 oz baby button mushrooms, quartered
50 g/2 oz peeled prawns, thawed if frozen
2 medium eggs, hard-boiled and chopped
450 g/1 lb ready-made puff pastry, thawed
    if frozen
1 small egg, beaten with a pinch of salt
assorted bitter salad leaves, to serve

Preheat the oven to 200°C/400°F/Gas Mark 6, 15 minutes before cooking. Place the fish in a shallow frying pan with the stock, 150 ml/¼ pint water and salt and pepper. Simmer for 8–10 minutes. Strain the fish, reserving the cooking liquor, and when cool enough to handle, flake into a bowl.

Melt the margarine or butter in a saucepan and cook the onions for 2–3 minutes, then add the rice, reserved fish liquor and dill. Season lightly. Cover and simmer for 10 minutes, then stir in the mushrooms and cook for a further 10 minutes, or until all the liquid is absorbed. Mix the rice with the cooked fish, prawns and eggs. Leave to cool.

Roll half the pastry out on a lightly floured surface into a 20 x 25 cm/8 x 10 inch rectangle. Place on a dampened baking sheet and arrange the fish mixture on top, leaving a 1 cm/½ inch border. Brush the border with a little water.

Roll out the remaining pastry to a rectangle the same size as before and use to cover the fish. Brush the edges lightly with a little of the beaten egg and press to seal. Roll out the pastry trimmings and use to decorate the top. Chill in the refrigerator for 30 minutes. Brush with the beaten egg and bake for 30 minutes, or until golden. Serve immediately with salad leaves.

Food Fact

Kulebyaka or *koulubiac* is a classic festive dish from Russia. It is traditionally made with a yeast dough, but ready-made puff pastry works well as an easy alternative.

Smoked Haddock Rosti

Ingredients (Serves 4)

450 g/1 lb potatoes, peeled and coarsely grated
1 large onion, peeled and coarsely grated
2–3 garlic cloves, peeled and crushed
300 g/10 oz smoked haddock
1 tbsp olive oil
salt and freshly ground black pepper
finely grated zest of ½ lemon
1 tbsp freshly chopped parsley
2 tbsp half-fat crème fraîche
lemon wedges, to serve
mixed salad leaves, to garnish

Dry the grated potatoes in a clean tea towel. Rinse the grated onion thoroughly in cold water, dry in a clean tea towel and add to the potatoes.

Stir the garlic into the potato mixture. Skin the smoked haddock and remove as many of the tiny pin bones as possible. Cut into thin slices and reserve.

Heat the oil in a nonstick frying pan. Add half the potatoes and press well down in the frying pan. Season to taste with salt and pepper.

Add a layer of fish and a sprinkling of lemon zest, parsley and a little black pepper.

Helpful Hint
Smoked mackerel would also work very well with this recipe.

Top with the remaining potatoes and press down firmly. Cover with a sheet of foil and cook on the lowest heat for 25–30 minutes.

Preheat the grill 2–3 minutes before the end of cooking time. Remove the foil and place the rosti under the grill to brown. Turn out on to a warmed serving dish and serve immediately with spoonfuls of crème fraîche, lemon wedges and mixed salad leaves.

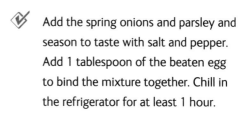

Tuna Fish Burgers

Ingredients (Makes 4)

450 g/1 lb potatoes, peeled and cut into chunks
40 g/ 1 ½ oz margarine or butter
2 tbsp milk
400 g can tuna in oil
1 spring onion, trimmed and finely chopped
1 tbsp freshly chopped parsley
salt and freshly ground black pepper
2 medium eggs, beaten
2 tbsp seasoned plain flour
125 g/4 oz fresh white breadcrumbs
4 tbsp vegetable oil
4 sesame seed baps (optional)

TO SERVE:
fat chips
mixed salad
tomato chutney

Place the potatoes in a large saucepan, cover with boiling water and simmer until soft. Drain, then mash with the margarine or butter and the milk. Turn into a large bowl. Drain the tuna, discarding the oil, and flake into the bowl of potato. Stir well to mix.

Add the spring onions and parsley and season to taste with salt and pepper. Add 1 tablespoon of the beaten egg to bind the mixture together. Chill in the refrigerator for at least 1 hour.

Shape the chilled mixture with your hands into four large burgers. Coat the burgers with seasoned flour, then brush them with the remaining beaten egg, allowing any excess to drip back into the bowl. Finally, coat them evenly in the breadcrumbs, pressing the crumbs on with your hands, if necessary.

Heat a little of the oil in a frying pan and fry the burgers for 2–3 minutes on each side until golden, adding more oil if necessary. Drain on kitchen paper and serve hot in baps, if using, with chips, mixed salad and chutney.

Helpful Hint
Dry the drained potatoes over a very low heat before mashing to ensure the mixture isn't too soft to shape. If possible, cover the uncooked coated burgers with clingfilm and chill in the refrigerator for 30 minutes so that they are really firm.

Salmon Fish Cakes

Ingredients (Serves 4)

350 g/12 oz salmon fillet, skinned
salt and freshly ground black pepper
450 g/1 lb potatoes, peeled and cut into chunks
25 g/1 oz margarine or butter
1 tbsp milk
2 medium tomatoes, skinned, deseeded and chopped
2 tbsp freshly chopped parsley
75 g/3 oz wholemeal breadcrumbs
2 tbsp plain flour
1 large egg, beaten
3–4 tbsp vegetable oil

TO SERVE:
ready-made raita
sprigs of fresh mint

 Place the salmon in a shallow frying pan and cover with water. Season to taste with salt and pepper and simmer for 8–10 minutes until the fish is cooked. Drain and flake into a bowl.

 Boil the potatoes in lightly salted water until soft, then drain. Mash with the margarine or butter and milk until smooth. Add the potato to the fish and stir in the tomatoes and half the parsley. Adjust the seasoning to taste. Chill the mixture in the refrigerator for at least 2 hours to firm up.

 Mix the breadcrumbs with the remaining parsley. When the fish mixture is firm, form into four flat cakes. First, lightly coat the fish cakes in the flour, then dip into the beaten egg, allowing any excess to drip back into the bowl. Finally, press into the breadcrumb mixture until well coated.

 Heat a little of the oil in a frying pan and fry the fish cakes in batches for 2–3 minutes on each side until golden and crisp, adding more oil if necessary. Serve with raita garnished with sprigs of mint.

Helpful Hint

To remove the skins from the tomatoes, pierce each with the tip of a sharp knife, then plunge into boiling water and leave for up to 1 minute. Drain, then rinse in cold water – the skins should peel off easily. Alternatively, hold them over a gas flame with a fork for a few seconds, turning until the skin is slightly blackened and blistered.

Spanish Omelette with Smoked Cod

Ingredients (Serves 3-4)

100 g/4 oz smoked cod
3 tbsp sunflower oil
350 g/12 oz potatoes, peeled and cut into
   1 cm/½ inch cubes
2 onions, peeled and cut into wedges
2–4 large garlic cloves, peeled and thinly sliced
1 large red pepper, deseeded, quartered and
   thinly sliced
25 g/1 oz margarine or butter, melted
6 eggs, beaten
salt and freshly ground black pepper
2 tbsp freshly chopped flat-leaf parsley
50 g/2 oz mature Cheddar cheese, grated

TO SERVE:
crusty bread
tossed green salad

Place the cod in a shallow dish and pour over boiling water. Leave for 5 minutes, then drain and allow to cool, When cool, discard the skin and any pin bones and cut into small pieces.

Heat the oil in a large nonstick heavy-based frying pan, add the potatoes, onions and garlic and cook gently for 10–15 minutes until golden brown, then add the red pepper. Place the cod on top of the vegetables and cook for 3 minutes.

When the vegetables are cooked, drain off any excess oil. Beat the margarine or butter into the eggs, season then stir in the parsley. Pour the egg mixture over the top of the vegetables and cod and cook gently for 5 minutes, or until the eggs become firm.

Sprinkle the grated cheese over the top and place the pan under a preheated hot grill. Cook for 2–3 minutes until the cheese is golden and bubbling. Carefully slide the omelette onto a large plate and serve immediately with plenty of bread and salad.

Pea and Prawn Risotto

Ingredients (Serves 4)

50 g/2 oz margarine or butter
1 red onion, peeled and chopped
4 garlic cloves, peeled and finely chopped
225 g/8 oz risotto rice
150 ml/¼ pint white wine, or use extra stock
1.1 litres/2 pints vegetable or fish stock, heated
225 g/8 oz prawns, peeled, and thawed if frozen
300 g/10 oz thawed frozen peas
4 tbsp freshly chopped mint
salt and freshly ground black pepper

Melt the margarine or butter in the pan and fry the onion and garlic for 5 minutes until softened, but not coloured. Add the rice and stir the grains in the butter for 1 minute, until they are coated thoroughly. Add the white wine or stock and boil rapidly until the wine or stock is reduced by half.

Add the heated stock to the rice, a ladleful at a time. Stir constantly, adding the stock as it is absorbed, until the rice is creamy, but still has a bite in the centre.

Stir the prawns into the rice, along with the peas. Add the chopped mint and season to taste with salt and pepper. Cover the pan and leave the prawns to infuse for 5 minutes before serving.

Helpful Hint
Ensure that the prawns are completely thawed before adding to the pan otherwise they will be tough to eat.

Fish Crumble

Ingredients (Serves 4)

350g/12oz whiting or pollack fillets
300 ml/½ pint milk
salt and freshly ground black pepper
1 tbsp sunflower oil
75 g/3 oz margarine or butter
1 medium onion, peeled and finely chopped
2 leeks, trimmed and sliced
1 medium carrot, peeled and cut into small dice
2 medium potatoes, peeled and cut into small pieces
175 g/6 oz plain flour
300 ml/½ pint fish or vegetable stock
1 tsp freshly chopped dill
runner beans, to serve

FOR THE CRUMBLE TOPPING:
75 g/3 oz margarine or butter
175 g/6 oz plain flour
25 g/1 oz Parmesan cheese, grated
¾ tsp cayenne pepper

 Preheat the oven to 200°C/400°F/Gas Mark 6, 15 minutes before cooking. Oil a 1.4 litre/2½ pint pie dish. Place the fish in a saucepan with the milk, salt

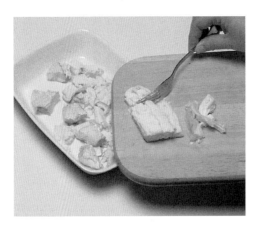

and pepper. Bring to the boil, cover and simmer for 8–10 minutes until the fish is cooked. Remove with a slotted spoon, reserving the cooking liquor. Flake the fish into the prepared dish.

 Heat the oil and 1 tablespoon of the margarine or butter in a small frying pan and gently fry the onion, leeks, carrot and potatoes for 1–2 minutes. Cover tightly and cook over a gentle heat for a further 10 minutes until softened. Spoon the vegetables over the fish.

 Melt the remaining margarine or butter in a saucepan, add the flour and cook for 1 minute, stirring. Whisk in the reserved cooking liquor and the stock. Cook until thickened. Remove from the heat and stir in the dill. Pour over the fish.

 To make the crumble, rub the margarine or butter into the flour until it resembles breadcrumbs, then stir in the cheese and cayenne pepper. Sprinkle over the dish, and bake in the preheated oven for 20 minutes until piping hot. Serve with runners.

Tasty Tip

Vary the taste and texture of the topping by making it with wholemeal flour, or by adding 25 g/1 oz chopped nuts or jumbo porridge oats.

Recipes: Pork

Bacon, Mushroom and Cheese Puffs

Ingredients (Serves 4)

1 tbsp olive oil
225 g/8 oz field mushrooms, wiped and roughly
   chopped
225 g/8 oz rindless streaky bacon, roughly chopped
2 tbsp freshly chopped parsley
salt and freshly ground black pepper
350 g/12 oz ready-rolled puff pastry sheets,
   thawed if frozen
25 g/1 oz Emmenthal cheese, grated
1 medium egg, beaten
salad leaves such as rocket or watercress, to garnish
tomatoes, to serve

Preheat the oven to 200°C/400°F/Gas Mark 6. Heat the olive oil in a large frying pan.

Add the mushrooms and bacon and fry for 6–8 minutes until golden in colour. Stir in the parsley, season to taste with salt and pepper and allow to cool.

Roll the sheet of pastry a little thinner on a lightly floured surface to a 30 cm/ 12 inch square. Cut the pastry into four equal squares.

Stir the grated Emmenthal cheese into the mushroom mixture. Spoon a quarter of the mixture on to one half of each square.

Brush the edges of the square with a little of the beaten egg.

Fold over the pastry to form a triangular parcel. Seal the edges well and place on a lightly oiled baking sheet. Repeat until all the squares are done.

Make shallow slashes in the top of the pastry with a knife.

Brush the parcels with the remaining beaten egg and cook in the preheated oven for 20 minutes, or until puffy and golden brown.

 Serve warm or cold, garnished with the salad leaves and served with tomatoes.

Tasty Tip

The Emmenthal cheese in this recipe can be substituted for any other cheese, but for best results use a cheese such as Cheddar, which, like Emmenthal, melts easily! The bacon can also be substituted for slices of sweeter cured hams such as pancetta, speck, Parma or prosciutto.

Potato Skins

Ingredients (Serves 4)

4 large baking potatoes
2 tbsp olive oil
2 tsp paprika
125 g/4 oz streaky bacon, roughly chopped
6 tbsp milk
125 g/4 oz Gorgonzola cheese
1 tbsp freshly chopped parsley

TO SERVE:
reduced-calorie mayonnaise
sweet chilli dipping sauce
tossed green salad

 Preheat the oven to 200°C/400°F/Gas Mark 6. Scrub the potatoes, then prick a few times with a fork or skewer and place directly on the top shelf of the oven. Bake in the preheated oven for at least 1 hour until tender. The potatoes are cooked when they yield gently to the pressure of your hand.

 Set the potatoes aside until cool enough to handle, then cut in half and scoop the flesh into a bowl and reserve. Preheat the grill and line the grill rack with foil.

 Mix together the oil and the paprika and use half to brush the outside of the potato skins. Place on the grill rack under the preheated hot grill and cook for 5 minutes, or until crisp, turning as necessary.

 Heat the remaining paprika-flavoured oil and gently fry the bacon until crisp. Add to the potato flesh along with the milk, Gorgonzola cheese and parsley. Halve the potato skins and fill with the Gorgonzola filling. Return to the oven for a further 15 minutes to heat through. Sprinkle with a little more paprika and serve immediately with mayonnaise, sweet chilli sauce and a green salad.

Helpful Hint

Use floury potatoes for this recipe such as King Edward or Maris Piper. Remove potatoes from the polythene bags and place in brown or cloth bags and leave in a cool dark dry place to ensure they last as long as possible.

Pork Goulash and Rice

Ingredients (Serves 4)

450 g/1lb boneless stewing pork, such as shoulder
1 tbsp olive oil
2 onions, peeled and roughly chopped
1 red pepper, deseeded and sliced thinly
1 garlic clove, peeled and crushed
1 tbsp plain flour
1 rounded tbsp paprika
400g can whole peeled tomatoes, chopped
salt and freshly ground black pepper
250 g/9 oz long-grain white rice
450 ml/¾ pint chicken stock, or use water
150 ml/¼ pint soured cream, to serve (optional)
fresh flat-leaf parsley sprigs, to garnish

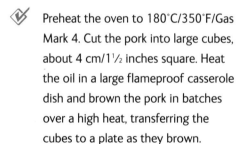

Preheat the oven to 180°C/350°F/Gas Mark 4. Cut the pork into large cubes, about 4 cm/1½ inches square. Heat the oil in a large flameproof casserole dish and brown the pork in batches over a high heat, transferring the cubes to a plate as they brown.

Over a medium heat, add the onions and pepper and cook for about 5 minutes, stirring regularly, until they begin to brown. Add the garlic and return the meat to the casserole along with any juices on the plate. Sprinkle in the flour and paprika and stir well to soak up the oil and juices.

Add the tomatoes and their liquor, then season to taste with salt and pepper. Bring slowly to the boil, cover with a tight-fitting lid and cook in the preheated oven for 1½ hours.

Meanwhile, rinse the rice in several changes of water until the water remains relatively clear. Drain well and put into a saucepan with the chicken stock or water and a little salt. Cover tightly and bring to the boil. Turn the heat down as low as possible and cook for 10 minutes without removing the lid. After this time, remove from the heat and leave for a further 10 minutes, without removing the lid. Fluff with a fork.

When the meat is tender, stir in the soured cream lightly to create a marbled effect, or serve separately. Garnish with parsley and serve immediately with the rice.

Nasi Goreng

Ingredients (Serves 4)

1 large onion, peeled
1 red chilli, deseeded and roughly chopped
2 garlic cloves, peeled and roughly chopped
4 tbsp sunflower oil
2 tsp tomato purée
2 tsp + 1 tbsp soy sauce
225 g/8 oz long-grain white rice
125 g/4 oz French beans, trimmed
3 medium eggs, beaten
pinch sugar
salt and freshly ground black pepper
125 g/4 oz cooked ham, shredded
75 g/3 oz cooked peeled prawns, thawed if frozen
6 spring onions, trimmed and thinly sliced
3 tbsp freshly chopped coriander

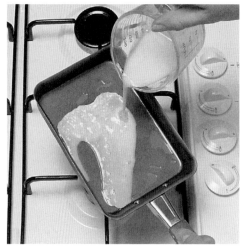

 Roughly chop a quarter of the onion and place with the red chilli, garlic, 1 tablespoon of the oil, tomato purée and 2 tsp soy sauce in a food processor and blend until smooth, then reserve. Boil the rice in plenty of salted water for 6–7 minutes until tender, adding the French beans after 4 minutes. Drain well and leave to cool.

 Beat the eggs with the sugar and a little salt and pepper. Heat a little of the oil in a small nonstick frying pan and add about one third of the egg mixture. Swirl to coat the base of the pan thinly and cook for about 1 minute until golden. Flip and cook the other side briefly before removing from the pan. Roll the omelette and slice thinly into strips. Repeat with the remaining egg mixture to make 3 omelettes.

Thinly slice the remaining onion then heat a further 2 tablespoons of the oil in a clean frying pan. Add the remaining onion to the pan and cook for 8–10 minutes over a medium heat until golden and crisp. Drain on absorbent kitchen paper and reserve.

Add the remaining 1 tablespoon of oil to a large wok or frying pan and fry the chilli paste over a medium heat for 1 minute. Add the cooked rice and beans and stir-fry for 2 minutes. Add the ham and prawns and continue stir-frying for a further 1–2 minutes. Add the omelette slices, half the fried onion, the spring onions, 1 tablespoon soy sauce and chopped coriander. Stir-fry for a further minute until heated through. Spoon onto serving plates and garnish with the remaining fried onion. Serve immediately.

Pork Sausages with Onion Gravy and Mash

Ingredients (Serves 4)

3 tbsp olive oil
2 large onions, peeled and thinly sliced
pinch sugar
1 tbsp freshly chopped thyme
1 tbsp plain flour
300 ml/½ pint vegetable stock
8–12 good-quality butcher's pork sausages,
   depending on size

FOR THE MASH:
700 g/1½ lb floury potatoes, peeled
25 g/1 oz margarine or butter
4 tbsp crème fraîche or soured cream
salt and freshly ground black pepper

Add the thyme, stir well, then add the flour, stirring. Gradually add the stock. Bring to the boil and simmer gently for 10 minutes.

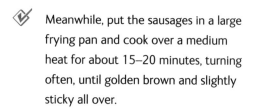

Meanwhile, put the sausages in a large frying pan and cook over a medium heat for about 15–20 minutes, turning often, until golden brown and slightly sticky all over.

For the mash, boil the potatoes in plenty of lightly salted water for

Heat the oil and add the onions. Cover and cook gently for about 20 minutes until the onions have collapsed. Add the sugar and stir well. Uncover and continue to cook, stirring often, until the onions are very soft and golden.

15–18 minutes until tender. Drain well and return to the saucepan. Put the saucepan over a low heat to allow the potatoes to dry thoroughly. Remove from the heat and add the margarine or butter, crème fraîche or soured cream and salt and pepper. Mash thoroughly. Serve the potato mash with the sausages and onion gravy.

Helpful Hint

Sausages should always be cooked slowly over a gentle heat to ensure that they are cooked through. There is a huge range of regional pork sausages to choose from.

Spanish Style Pork Stew with Saffron Rice

Ingredients (Serves 4)

2 tbsp olive oil
450 g/1 lb boneless pork shoulder, diced
1 large onion, peeled and sliced
2 garlic cloves, peeled and finely chopped
1 tbsp plain flour
400 g can whole peeled tomatoes, chopped
175 ml/6 fl oz chicken stock, or use red wine
1 tbsp freshly chopped basil
1 green pepper, deseeded and sliced
25 g/1oz pimiento-stuffed olives, cut in half crossways
salt and freshly ground black pepper
fresh basil leaves, to garnish

FOR THE SAFFRON RICE:
1 tbsp olive oil
small knob margarine or butter (optional)
1 small onion, peeled and finely chopped
few strands saffron, crushed
250 g/9 oz long-grain white rice
600 ml/1 pint chicken stock

Preheat the oven to 180°C/350°F/Gas Mark 4. Heat the oil in a large flameproof casserole dish and add the pork in batches. Fry over a high heat until browned. Transfer to a plate and repeat until all the pork is browned.

Lower the heat and add the onion to the casserole dish. Cook for a further 5 minutes until soft and starting to brown. Add the garlic and stir briefly before returning the pork to the casserole. Add the flour and stir.

Add the tomatoes. Gradually stir in the stock or wine and add the basil. Bring to simmering point and cover. Transfer the dish to the lower part of the preheated oven and cook for 1½ hours. Stir in the green pepper and olives and cook for 30 minutes. Season to taste with salt and pepper.

Meanwhile, to make the saffron rice, heat the oil with the margarine or butter in a saucepan. Add the onion and cook for 5 minutes over a medium heat until softened. Add the saffron and rice and stir well. Add the stock, bring to the boil, cover and reduce the heat as low as possible. Cook for 15 minutes, covered, until the rice is tender and the stock is absorbed. Adjust the seasoning and serve with the stew, garnished with fresh basil leaves.

Gnocchetti with Broccoli and Bacon Sauce

Ingredients (Serves 4)

350 g/12 oz broccoli florets
3 tbsp olive oil
50 g/2 oz streaky bacon, finely chopped
1 small onion, peeled and finely chopped
3 garlic cloves, peeled and sliced
200 ml/7 fl oz milk
350 g/12 oz gnocchetti (little ribbed pasta shells)
25 g/1 oz freshly grated Parmesan cheese, plus extra
   to serve
salt and freshly ground black pepper

Bring a large pan of salted water to the boil. Add the broccoli florets and cook for about 8–10 minutes until very soft. Drain thoroughly, allow to cool slightly, then chop finely and reserve.

Heat the olive oil in a heavy-based pan, add the bacon and cook over a medium heat for 5 minutes, or until golden and crisp. Add the onion and cook for a further 5 minutes, or until soft and lightly golden. Add the garlic and cook for 1 minute.

Transfer the chopped broccoli to the bacon mixture and pour in the milk. Bring slowly to the boil and simmer rapidly for about 15 minutes until reduced to a creamy texture.

Meanwhile, bring a large pan of lightly salted water to a rolling boil. Add the pasta and cook according to the packet instructions, or until *al dente*.

Drain the pasta thoroughly, reserving a little of the cooking water. Add the pasta and the Parmesan cheese to the broccoli mixture. Toss, adding enough of the reserved cooking water to make a creamy sauce. Season to taste with salt and pepper. Serve immediately with extra Parmesan cheese.

Fettuccine with Mushrooms and Prosciutto

Ingredients (Serves 4)

2 tbsp olive oil
1 small onion, peeled and finely chopped
2 garlic cloves, peeled and finely chopped
4 slices prosciutto, chopped or torn
225 g/8 oz mushrooms, wiped if necessary and sliced
350 g/12 oz fettuccine
3 tbsp crème fraîche
2 tbsp freshly chopped parsley
salt and freshly ground black pepper
freshly grated Parmesan cheese, to serve (optional)

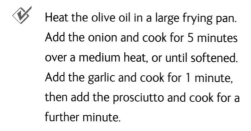 Heat the olive oil in a large frying pan. Add the onion and cook for 5 minutes over a medium heat, or until softened. Add the garlic and cook for 1 minute, then add the prosciutto and cook for a further minute.

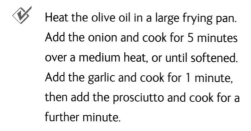 Add the sliced mushrooms to the pan and cook for 2-3 minutes stirring frequently.

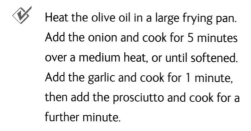 Meanwhile, bring a large pan of lightly salted water to a rolling boil. Add the pasta and cook according to the packet instructions, or until *al dente*.

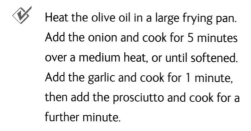 Stir the crème fraîche and chopped parsley into the mushroom mixture and heat through gently. Season to taste with salt and pepper. Drain the pasta well, transfer to a large warmed serving dish and pour over the sauce. Serve immediately with grated Parmesan cheese.

Food Fact
Prosciutto is produced from pigs fed on whey, a by-product of the local Parmesan cheese industry. The ham is dry cured, then weighted to flatten it and give it a dense texture. The delicious flavour develops during the year it is allowed to mature. It is always served in paper-thin slices, either raw or lightly fried.

Italian Risotto

Ingredients (Serves 4)

1 onion, peeled
2 garlic cloves, peeled
1 tbsp olive oil
125 g/4 oz Italian salami or speck, chopped
125 g/4 oz asparagus
350 g/12 oz risotto rice
1.2 litres/2 pints chicken stock, warmed
125g/4 oz frozen broad beans, defrosted
75 g/3 oz Dolcelatte cheese, diced
3 tbsp freshly chopped mixed herbs, such as parsley
  and basil
salt and freshly ground black pepper

 Chop the onion and garlic and reserve. Heat the olive oil in a large frying pan and cook the salami for 3–5 minutes until golden. Using a slotted spoon, transfer to a plate and keep warm. Add the asparagus to the pan and stir-fry for 2–3 minutes, until just wilted. Transfer to the plate with the salami. Add the onion and garlic to the pan and cook for 5 minutes, or until softened.

 Add the rice to the pan and cook for about 2 minutes. Add 300 ml/½ pint of the stock and bring to the boil, then simmer, stirring, until the stock has been absorbed. Add a further 450 ml/¾ pint of the stock and return to the boil. Simmer, stirring, until the liquid has been absorbed.

 Add a further 300ml/½ pint of the stock and the broad beans to the rice mixture. Bring to the boil, then simmer for a further 5–10 minutes until all of the liquid has been absorbed.

 Add the remaining stock, bring to the boil, then simmer until all the liquid is absorbed and the rice is tender. Add the remaining ingredients and stir until the cheese has just melted. Serve immediately.

Food Fact
Cheese is a common constituent in the making of risotto and in fact helps to provide some of its creamy texture. Usually Parmesan cheese is added at the end of cooking but here a good-quality Dolcelatte is used instead.

Oven-baked Pork Balls with Peppers

Ingredients (Serves 4)

350 g/12 oz fresh pork mince
4 tbsp freshly chopped basil
2 garlic cloves, peeled and chopped
salt and freshly ground black pepper
3 tbsp olive oil
1 medium red pepper, deseeded and cut into chunks
1 medium green pepper, deseeded and cut into chunks
1 medium yellow pepper, deseeded and cut
  into chunks
125 g/4 oz cherry tomatoes
2 tbsp balsamic vinegar
garlic bread, to serve

 Preheat the oven to 200°C/400°F/Gas Mark 6, 15 minutes before cooking. Mix together the pork, basil, 1 chopped garlic clove and seasoning until well combined. With damp hands, divide the mixture into 16, then roll into balls and reserve.

 Spoon the olive oil into a large roasting tin and place in the preheated oven for about 3 minutes until very hot. Remove from the heat and add the pork balls, the remaining chopped garlic and the peppers. Bake for about 15 minutes. Remove from the oven, add the cherry tomatoes and season to taste with salt and pepper. Bake for a further 20 minutes.

Remove the pork balls from the oven, stir in the vinegar and serve immediately with garlic bread if liked.

Helpful Hint
Look for large bags of frozen garlic bread – that way you only need to use the right amount and will have plenty left for other meals.

Tagliatelle with Spicy Sausage Ragu

Ingredients (Serves 4)

3 tbsp olive oil
4 spicy sausages
1 small onion, peeled and finely chopped
1–2 garlic cloves, peeled and crushed
1 tsp fennel seeds
175 g/6 oz fresh pork mince
225 g/8 oz canned whole peeled tomatoes,
    chopped, plus 2 tbsp of the tomato liquor
1 tbsp tomato purée
salt and freshly ground black pepper
350 g/12 oz tagliatelle
300 ml/¹/₂ pint prepared white sauce
25 g/1 oz freshly grated Parmesan cheese

 Preheat the oven to 200°C/400°F/Gas Mark 6, 15 minutes before cooking. Heat 1 tablespoon of the olive oil in a large frying pan. Prick the sausages, add to the pan and cook for 8–10 minutes, or until browned and cooked through. Remove and cut into thin diagonal slices. Reserve.

 Return the pan to the heat and pour in the remaining olive oil. Add the onion and garlic and cook for 8 minutes, or until softened. Add the fennel seeds and minced pork and cook, stirring, for 5–8 minutes until the meat is sealed and browned.

 Stir in the tomatoes with their liquor and the tomato purée. Season to taste with salt and pepper. Bring to the boil, cover and simmer for 30 minutes, stirring occasionally. Remove the lid and simmer for 10 minutes.

 Bring a large pan of lightly salted water to a rolling boil. Add the pasta and cook according to the packet instructions, or until *al dente*. Drain thoroughly and toss with the meat sauce.

 Place half the pasta in an ovenproof dish and cover with 4 tablespoons of the white sauce. Top with half the sausages and grated Parmesan cheese. Repeat the layering, finishing with white sauce and Parmesan cheese. Bake in the preheated oven for 20 minutes, until golden brown. Serve immediately.

Bacon and Rigatoni Supper

Ingredients (Serves 4)

25 g/1 oz margarine or butter
2 tbsp olive oil
2 large onions, peeled and finely sliced
1 tsp soft brown sugar
2 garlic cloves, peeled and crushed
225 g/8 oz streaky bacon, sliced
1 chilli, deseeded and finely sliced
400g can whole peeled tomatoes, chopped
1 tbsp tomato purée
150 ml/¼ pint pork or chicken stock
salt and freshly ground black pepper
450 g/1 lb rigatoni
freshly chopped parsley, to garnish

 Melt the margarine or butter with the olive oil in a large heavy-based pan. Add the onions and sugar and cook over a very low heat, stirring occasionally, for 15 minutes, or until soft and starting to caramelise.

 Add the garlic and bacon to the pan and cook for 5 minutes. Stir in the chilli, chopped tomatoes and tomato purée, then pour in the stock. Season well with salt and pepper. Bring to the boil, cover, reduce the heat and simmer for 30 minutes, stirring occasionally. Remove the lid and simmer for a further 10 minutes, or until the sauce starts to thicken.

 Meanwhile, bring a large pan of lightly salted water to a rolling boil. Add the pasta and cook according to the packet instructions, or until *al dente*.

 Drain the pasta, reserving 2 tablespoons of the water, and return to the pan. Add the bacon sauce with the reserved cooking water and toss gently until the pasta is evenly covered. Tip into a warmed serving dish, sprinkle with the parsley and serve immediately.

Helpful Hint
Although there are many different types of chilli, they all have a hot, spicy flavour. Take care when preparing chillies as the volatile oils in the seeds and the membrane can cause irritation – wash your hands thoroughly afterwards.

Pork Fried Noodles

Ingredients (Serves 4)

125 g/4 oz dried thread egg noodles
125 g/4 oz broccoli florets
2 tbsp groundnut oil
300 g/10 oz pork tenderloin, cut into slices
3 tbsp soy sauce
1 tbsp lemon juice
pinch sugar
1 tsp chilli sauce
2.5 cm/1 inch piece fresh root ginger, peeled and cut
     into sticks
1 garlic clove, peeled and chopped
1 green chilli, deseeded and sliced
25 g/1 oz mangetout, halved
2 medium eggs, lightly beaten

TO GARNISH:
radish rose
spring onion curls

Place the noodles in a bowl and cover with boiling water. Leave to stand for 20 minutes, stirring occasionally, or until tender. Drain and reserve. Meanwhile, blanch the broccoli in a saucepan of lightly salted boiling water for 2 minutes. Drain, refresh under cold running water and reserve.

Heat a large wok or frying pan, add the groundnut oil and heat until just smoking. Add the pork and stir-fry for 5 minutes, or until browned. Using a slotted spoon, remove the pork slices and reserve.

Mix together the soy sauce, lemon juice, sugar and chilli sauce; reserve.

Add the ginger to the wok and stir-fry for 30 seconds. Add the garlic and chilli and stir-fry for 30 seconds. Add the reserved broccoli and stir-fry for 3 minutes. Stir in the mangetout, pork and reserved noodles with the beaten eggs. Stir-fry for 5 minutes or until heated through. Pour over the reserved sauce, toss well and turn into a warmed serving dish. Garnish and serve immediately.

Singapore Noodles

Ingredients (Serves 4)

225 g/8 oz vermicelli rice noodles
2 tbsp vegetable oil
2 shallots, peeled and sliced
2 garlic cloves, peeled and crushed
2 tbsp freshly grated root ginger
1 red pepper, deseeded and
   finely sliced
1 red bird's eye chilli, deseeded and finely chopped
100 g/4 oz boneless lean pork, diced
125 g/4 oz boneless chicken, diced
1 tbsp curry powder
1 tsp each crushed fennel seeds and ground cinnamon
125 g/4 oz cooked peeled prawns, thawed if frozen
50 g/2 oz frozen peas, thawed
juice of 1 lemon
3 tbsp fresh coriander leaves

 Put the noodles into a large bowl and pour over boiling water to cover. Leave to stand for 3 minutes, or until slightly underdone according to the packet instructions. Drain well and reserve.

 Heat a wok until almost smoking. Add the oil and carefully swirl around to coat the sides of the wok. Add the shallots, garlic and ginger and cook for a few seconds. Add the pepper and chilli and stir-fry for 3–4 minutes until the pepper has softened.

 Add the pork, chicken and curry powder to the wok. Stir-fry for a further 4–5 minutes until the meat is sealed on all sides, then add the fennel seeds and the ground cinnamon and stir to mix.

Add the drained noodles to the wok along with the prawns and peas and cook for a further 2–4 minutes until heated through. Add the lemon juice to taste. Sprinkle with the fresh coriander leaves and serve immediately.

Helpful Hint
This is also a great dish for using up leftover meat, perhaps from the Sunday roast. If using cooked meat, reduce the cooking time accordingly, but make sure that it is piping hot.

Oven-roasted Vegetables with Sausages

Ingredients (Serves 4)

3 tbsp olive oil
1 aubergine, trimmed and cut into bite-sized chunks
3 courgettes, trimmed and cut into bite-sized chunks
6 garlic cloves, unpeeled
8 Tuscany-style sausages
4 plum tomatoes
300 g/10 oz can cannellini beans
salt and freshly ground black pepper
1 small bunch fresh basil, torn into coarse pieces
4 tbsp freshly grated Parmesan cheese

Preheat the oven to 200°C/400°F/Gas Mark 6, 15 minutes before cooking. Line a large roasting tin with foil and pour in the olive oil, then heat in the preheated oven for 3 minutes, or until very hot. Add the aubergine, courgettes and garlic cloves, then stir until coated in the hot oil and cook in the oven for 10 minutes.

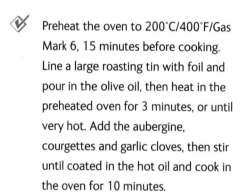

Remove the roasting tin from the oven and stir the vegetables. Lightly prick the sausages, add to the roasting tin and return to the oven. Continue to roast for a further 20 minutes, turning once during cooking, until the vegetables are tender and the sausages are golden brown.

Meanwhile, roughly chop the plum tomatoes and drain, then rinse, the cannellini beans. Remove the roasting tin from the oven and stir in the tomatoes and cannellini beans. Season to taste with salt and pepper, then return to the oven for 5 minutes, or until heated thoroughly.

Scatter over the basil leaves and sprinkle with plenty of Parmesan cheese and freshly ground black pepper. Serve immediately.

Helpful Hint
By leaving the garlic cloves unpeeled, a more delicate flavour is achieved. If a more robust flavour is required, peel the garlic before cooking.

Risi e Bisi

Ingredients (Serves 4)

25 g/1 oz margarine or butter
1 tsp olive oil
3 rashers streaky bacon, chopped
1 small onion, peeled and finely chopped
1 garlic clove, peeled and finely chopped
pinch caster sugar
1 tsp lemon juice
1 bay leaf
1.25 litres/2¼ pints vegetable stock
200 g/7 oz risotto rice
175 g/6 oz frozen petits pois, thawed
3 tbsp freshly chopped parsley
25 g/1oz Parmesan cheese, finely grated
salt and freshly ground black pepper
julienne strips orange zest, to garnish

Melt the margarine or butter and olive oil together in a large heavy-based saucepan. Add the chopped bacon, the chopped onion and garlic and gently fry for about 10 minutes until the onion is softened and is just beginning to colour.

Add the caster sugar, lemon juice and bay leaf, then pour in the vegetable stock. Bring the mixture to a fast boil.

Add the rice, stir and simmer, uncovered, for about 20 minutes until the rice is tender. Occasionally, stir the mixture gently while it cooks.

Add the petits pois and stir them into the rice about 2 minutes before the end of the cooking time.

When the rice is cooked, remove the bay leaf and discard. Stir in 2½ tablespoons of the chopped parsley and the grated Parmesan cheese. Season to taste with salt and pepper.

Transfer the rice to a large serving dish. Garnish with the remaining chopped parsley and the strips of orange zest. Serve immediately while piping hot.

Cassoulet

Ingredients (Serves 4)

1 tbsp olive oil
1 onion, peeled and chopped
2 celery stalks, trimmed and chopped
175 g/6 oz carrots, peeled and sliced
2–3 garlic cloves, peeled and crushed
350 g/12 oz pork belly (optional)
8 spicy thick sausages, such as Toulouse
few fresh thyme sprigs
salt and freshly ground black pepper
2 x 400 g cans cannellini beans,
    drained and rinsed
600 ml/1 pint vegetable stock
75 g/3 oz fresh breadcrumbs
2 tbsp freshly chopped thyme

if using, into small pieces and cut the sausages into chunks.

Add the meat to the vegetables and cook, stirring, until lightly browned.

Add the thyme sprigs and season to taste with salt and pepper. If a saucepan was used, transfer everything to an ovenproof casserole dish.

Preheat the oven to 180°C/350°F/Gas Mark 4. Heat the oil in a large saucepan or ovenproof casserole dish, add the onion, celery, carrot and garlic and sauté for 5 minutes. Cut the pork,

Spoon the beans on top, then pour in the stock. Mix the breadcrumbs with 1 tablespoon of the chopped thyme in a small bowl and sprinkle on top of the beans. Cover with a lid and cook in the oven for 40 minutes. Remove the lid and cook for a further 15 minutes, or until the breadcrumbs are crisp. Sprinkle with the remaining chopped thyme and serve.

Tasty Tip

Replace the pork belly with lardons, if you prefer.

Leek and Ham Risotto

Ingredients (Serves 4)

1 tbsp olive oil
25 g/1 oz margarine or butter
1 onion, peeled and finely chopped
3 leeks, trimmed and thinly sliced
1½ tbsp freshly chopped thyme
350 g/12 oz risotto rice
1.5 litres/2½ pints vegetable or
   chicken stock, heated
175 g/6 oz cooked ham
125 g/4 oz peas, thawed if frozen
25 g/1oz Parmesan cheese, grated
salt and freshly ground black pepper

Heat the oil and half the margarine or butter together in a large saucepan. Add the onion and leeks and cook over a medium heat for 6–8 minutes, stirring occasionally, until soft and beginning to colour. Stir in the thyme and cook briefly.

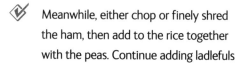

Add the rice and stir well. Continue stirring over a medium heat for about 1 minute until the rice is glossy. Add a ladleful or two of the stock and stir well until the stock is absorbed. Continue adding stock, a ladleful at a time, and stirring well between additions, until about two thirds of the stock has been added.

Meanwhile, either chop or finely shred the ham, then add to the rice together with the peas. Continue adding ladlefuls

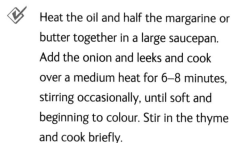

of stock, as described in the previous step, until the rice is tender and the ham is heated through thoroughly.

Add the remaining margarine or butter, sprinkle over the Parmesan cheese and season to taste with salt and pepper. When the cheese has softened, stir well to blend. Taste and adjust the seasoning, then serve immediately.

Helpful Hint
Risotto should take about 20-25 minutes to cook, so taste it after this time – the rice should be creamy with just a slight bite to it. If it is not quite ready, continue adding the stock, a little at a time, and cook for a few more minutes. Stop as soon as it tastes ready, as you do not have to add all of the liquid.

Recipes: Beef

Chilli Beef Calzone

Ingredients (Serves 4)

FOR THE BASIC PIZZA DOUGH:
225 g/8 oz strong plain flour
$^1/_2$ tsp salt
$^1/_4$ tsp quick-acting dried yeast
150 ml/$^1/_4$ pint warm water
1 tbsp olive oil

FOR THE FILLING:
1 tbsp sunflower oil
1 onion, peeled and finely chopped
1 green pepper, deseeded and chopped
225 g/8 oz fresh lean beef mince
420 g can chilli beans
200g/7oz whole canned tomatoes, chopped

mixed salad leaves, to serve

Preheat the oven to 220°C/425°F/Gas Mark 7, 15 minutes before baking. Sift the flour and salt into a bowl and stir in the yeast. Make a well in the centre and gradually add the water and oil to form a soft dough.

Knead the dough on a floured surface for about 5 minutes until smooth and elastic. Place in a lightly oiled bowl and cover with clingfilm. Leave to rise in a warm place for 1 hour.

Heat the oil in a large saucepan and gently cook the onion and pepper for 5 minutes.

Add the beef mince to the saucepan and cook for 10 minutes, until browned.

Add the chilli beans and tomatoes and simmer gently for 30 minutes, or until the mince is tender. Place a baking sheet into the preheated oven to heat up.

Knock the pizza dough with your fist a few times, then divide into four equal pieces. Cover three pieces of the dough with clingfilm and roll out the other piece on a lightly floured board to a 20 cm/8 inch round.

Spoon a quarter of the chilli mixture on to half of the dough round and dampen the edges with a little water.

Fold over the empty half of the dough and press the edges together well to seal.

Repeat this process with the remaining dough. Place on the hot baking sheet and bake for 15 minutes. Serve with the salad leaves.

Tasty Tip

Calzone is a stuffed pizza which originates from Naples. For a vegetarian version, replace the meat with sliced roasted vegetables such as peppers, onions, courgettes, mushrooms and aubergines. Sprinkle some grated mozzarella cheese over the vegetables and fold the dough over into a half-moon shape as in the recipe method. Serve with tomato sauce on the side.

Cornish Pasties

Ingredients (Makes 4)

FOR THE PASTRY:
225 g/8 oz self-raising flour
50 g/2 oz margarine or butter
50 g/2 oz white vegetable fat
salt and freshly ground black pepper

FOR THE FILLING:
225 g/8 oz lb braising steak, chopped very finely
1 medium onion, peeled and finely chopped
1 medium potato, peeled and diced
125 g/4 oz swede, peeled and diced
1–2 tbsp Worcestershire sauce, or to taste
1 small egg, beaten, to glaze

TO GARNISH:
tomato slices or wedges
fresh parsley sprigs

Preheat the oven to 180°C/350°F/Gas Mark 4, about 15 minutes before required. To make the pastry, sift the flour into a large bowl and add the fats, chopped into little pieces. Rub the fats and flour together until the mixture resembles coarse breadcrumbs. Season to taste with salt and pepper and mix again.

Add about 1–2 tablespoons of cold water, a little at a time, and mix until the mixture comes together to form a firm but pliable dough. Turn onto a lightly floured surface, knead until smooth, then wrap and chill in the refrigerator.

To make the filling, put the steak in a large bowl with the onion. Add the potatoes and swede to the bowl together with the Worcestershire sauce and salt and pepper. Mix well.

Divide the dough into four balls and roll each ball into a circle about 25 cm/ 10 inches across. Divide the filling between the circles of pastry. Wet the edge of the pastry, then fold over the filling. Pinch the edges to seal.

Transfer the pasties to a lightly oiled baking sheet. Make a couple of small holes in each pasty and brush with beaten egg. Cook in the preheated oven for 15 minutes, remove and brush again with the egg. Return to the oven for a further 15–20 minutes until golden. Cool slightly, garnish with tomato and parsley and serve.

Cottage Pie

Ingredients (Serves 4)

350 g/12 oz lean fresh beef mince
2 tbsp vegetable or olive oil
1 onion, peeled and finely chopped
1 carrot, peeled and finely chopped
1 celery stalk, trimmed and finely chopped
1 tbsp fresh thyme leaves
300 ml/½ pint beef or vegetable stock
   or leftover gravy
2 tbsp tomato purée
salt and freshly ground black pepper
700 g/1½ lb potatoes, peeled and cut into chunks
25 g/1 oz margarine or butter
6 tbsp milk
1 tbsp freshly chopped parsley
fresh herbs, to garnish

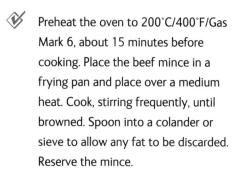

Preheat the oven to 200°C/400°F/Gas Mark 6, about 15 minutes before cooking. Place the beef mince in a frying pan and place over a medium heat. Cook, stirring frequently, until browned. Spoon into a colander or sieve to allow any fat to be discarded. Reserve the mince.

Wipe the frying pan clean then heat the oil and add the onion, carrot and celery. Cook over a medium heat for 8–10 minutes until softened and starting to brown.

Add the thyme and cook briefly, then return the beef mince to the pan together with the stock or gravy and tomato purée. Season to taste with salt and pepper and simmer gently for 25–30 minutes until reduced and thickened. Remove from the heat to cool slightly and check seasoning.

Meanwhile, boil the potatoes in plenty of salted water for 12–15 minutes until tender. Drain and return to the saucepan over a low heat to dry out. Remove from the heat and add the margarine or butter, milk and parsley. Mash until creamy, adding a little more milk if necessary. Adjust the seasoning.

Transfer the beef mixture to a shallow ovenproof dish. Spoon the mash over the filling and spread evenly to cover completely. Fork the surface, place on a baking sheet, then cook in the preheated oven for 25–30 minutes until the potato topping is browned and the filling is piping hot. Garnish and serve.

Gnocchi with Tuscan Beef Ragu

Ingredients (Serves 4)

3 tbsp olive oil
1 small onion, peeled and finely chopped
1 carrot, peeled and finely chopped
1 celery stalk, trimmed and finely chopped
1 fennel bulb, trimmed and sliced
2 garlic cloves, peeled and crushed
450 g/1 lb fresh lean beef mince
1 tbsp freshly chopped rosemary
2 tbsp tomato purée
50 ml/2 fl oz beef stock
400 g/14 oz can whole peeled tomatoes, chopped
225 g/8 oz fresh gnocchi
50 g/2 oz mozzarella cheese, cubed
salt and freshly ground black pepper

Preheat the oven to 200°C/400°F/Gas Mark 6, 15 minutes before cooking.

Heat the olive oil in a large heavy-based pan. Add the onion, carrot, celery, fennel and garlic and cook for 8 minutes, stirring, or until soft. Add the beef mince and cook, stirring, for 5–8 minutes until browned and any lumps are broken up.

Add the rosemary, tomato purée, stock and chopped tomatoes and simmer gently for about 40 minutes, stirring occasionally.

Meanwhile, bring 1.7 litres/3 pints of lightly salted water to a rolling boil in a large pan. Add the gnocchi and cook for 1–2 minutes until they rise to the surface.

Drain the gnocchi and place in an ovenproof dish. Stir in three quarters of the mozzarella cheese with the beef sauce; season. Top with the remaining mozzarella. Bake in the preheated oven for 20 minutes, until golden brown. Serve immediately.

Meatballs with Olives

Ingredients (Serves 4)

1 large onion, peeled
2–3 garlic cloves, peeled
350 g/12 oz fresh lean beef mince
2 tbsp fresh white or wholemeal breadcrumbs
3 tbsp freshly chopped basil
salt and freshly ground black pepper
2 tbsp olive oil
5 tbsp ready-made pesto
50 g/2 oz mascarpone cheese, chopped or grated
25 g/1 oz pitted black olives, halved
275 g/10 oz thick pasta noodles
freshly chopped flat-leaf parsley
fresh flat-leaf parsley sprigs, to garnish
freshly grated Parmesan cheese, to serve (optional)

Chop a quarter of the onion finely and place in a bowl with the garlic, beef mince, breadcrumbs, basil and seasoning to taste. With damp hands, bring the mixture together and shape into small balls about the size of an apricot.

Heat the olive oil in a frying pan and cook the meatballs for 8–10 minutes, turning occasionally, until browned and the beef is tender. Remove and drain on absorbent kitchen paper.

Slice the remaining onion, add to the pan and cook for 5 minutes, until softened. Blend the pesto and mascarpone together, then stir into the pan with the olives. Bring to the boil, reduce the heat and return the meatballs to the pan. Simmer for 5–8 minutes until the sauce has thickened and the meatballs are cooked thoroughly.

Meanwhile, bring a large saucepan of lightly salted water to the boil and cook the noodles for 8–10 minutes *al dente*. Drain the noodles, reserving 2 tablespoons of the cooking liquor. Return the noodles to the pan with the cooking liquor and pour in the sauce. Stir the noodles, then sprinkle with chopped parsley. Garnish with a few parsley sprigs and serve immediately with grated Parmesan cheese.

Helpful Hint

To stone olives, make a cut lengthways around the olive, then place on a chopping board with the cut facing upwards. Put the side of the knife (with the blade facing away from you) on top of the olive and tap sharply with the heel of your hand. The stone should come away, leaving the olive in two pieces.

Steak and Kidney Stew

Ingredients (Serves 4)

1 tbsp olive oil
1 onion, peeled and chopped
2–3 garlic cloves, peeled and crushed
2 celery stalks, trimmed and sliced
450 g/1 lb stewing steak, trimmed and diced
2-4 lambs' kidneys, cored and chopped
2 tbsp plain flour
1 tbsp tomato purée
900 ml/1½ pints beef stock
salt and freshly ground black pepper
1 fresh bay leaf
2 large carrots, peeled and sliced
350 g/12 oz new potatoes, scrubbed and cut in
   half or quarters if large
225 g/8 oz fresh spinach leaves, chopped

FOR THE DUMPLINGS:
125 g/4 oz self-raising flour
50 g/2 oz shredded suet
1 tbsp freshly chopped mixed herbs
2–3 tbsp water

Heat the oil in a large, heavy-based saucepan, add the onion, garlic and celery and sauté for 5 minutes, or until browned. Remove from the pan with a slotted spoon and reserve.

Add the steak and kidneys to the pan and cook for 3–5 minutes until sealed, then return the onion mixture to the pan. Sprinkle in the flour and cook, stirring, for 2 minutes. Take off the heat, stir in the tomato purée, then the stock, and season to taste with salt and pepper. Add the bay leaf.

Return to the heat and bring to the boil, stirring occasionally. Add the carrots, then reduce the heat to a simmer and cover with a lid. Cook for 1½ hours, stirring occasionally. Reduce the heat if the liquid is evaporating quickly. Add the potatoes and cook for a further 30 minutes.

Place the flour, suet and herbs in a bowl and add a little seasoning. Add the water and mix to a stiff mixture. Using a little extra flour, shape into eight small balls. Place the dumplings on top of the stew, cover with the lid and continue to cook for 15 minutes, or until the meat is tender and the dumplings are well risen and fluffy. Stir in the spinach and leave to stand for 2 minutes, or until the spinach is wilted.

Sausage and Apple Pot

Ingredients (Serves 4)

1 tbsp olive oil
1 onion, peeled and sliced
2–3 garlic cloves, peeled and sliced
2 celery sticks, trimmed and sliced
8 large beef sausages
300 g/10 oz carrots, peeled and sliced
1 large cooking apple, peeled and sliced
300 g/10 oz courgettes, trimmed and sliced
salt and freshly ground black pepper
600 ml/1 pint vegetable stock
2 tsp dried mixed herbs
450 g/1 lb potatoes, peeled and grated
2 tbsp Gruyère cheese, grated

Preheat the oven to 180°C/350°F/Gas Mark 4. Heat the oil in an ovenproof casserole dish (or frying pan, if preferred), add the onion, garlic and celery and sauté for 5 minutes. Push the vegetables to one side, then add the sausages and cook, turning the sausages over, until browned.

Transfer everything to a casserole dish. Arrange the onions over and around the sausages together with the carrots, apple and courgettes. Season to taste with salt and pepper and pour over the stock. Sprinkle with the mixed herbs, cover with a lid and cook in the oven for 30 minutes.

Meanwhile, soak the grated potatoes in a bowl of cold water for 10 minutes. Drain thoroughly, then place the potatoes on a clean tea towel and squeeze to remove any excess moisture.

Remove the casserole from the oven and place the grated potatoes on top. Sprinkle with the grated cheese, then return to the oven and cook for 30 minutes, or until the vegetables are tender and the topping is crisp.

Helpful Hint

When using the oven to cook a meal, try and cook other food at the same time so as to save on power bills. Cook small cakes or biscuits when cooking for 30 minutes. When cooking casseroles or stews in the oven, cook rice pudding or other puddings such as bread and butter pudding.

Thai Beef Curry

Ingredients (Serves 4)

450 g/1 lb stewing beef
1 tbsp vegetable oil
1–2 tbsp Thai green curry paste, or to taste
2 onions, peeled and chopped
2 tbsp lime juice
450 ml/³⁄₄ pint beef stock
150 ml/¹⁄₄ pint coconut milk
1 tsp soy sauce
1–2 tsp sugar
2 tbsp freshly chopped coriander
freshly cooked egg noodles, to serve

 Trim the beef, discarding any fat and gristle, cut into bite-sized chunks and reserve. Heat the oil in a heavy-based saucepan. Add the Thai green curry paste and onions and fry for 5 minutes, or until the onion has begun to soften.

 Add the beef to the pan and continue to fry for a further 5 minutes, or until sealed and lightly coated in the paste.

 Pour in the lime juice, stock and coconut milk, then add the soy sauce. Stir and add the sugar. Bring to the boil, reduce the heat, cover and simmer, stirring occasionally, for 2 hours, or until the meat is tender. Check the level of liquid during cooking and if it is evaporating too quickly, add some more beef stock and reduce the heat. Sprinkle with chopped coriander and serve with freshly cooked noodles.

Helpful Hint

When using small amounts of coconut milk, look for the blocks of creamed coconut that dissolve in hot water. To produce the equivalent of 300 ml/¹⁄₂ pint coconut milk, dissolve 25 g/1 oz creamed coconut in 275 ml/9 fl oz boiling water. If a thicker milk or cream is required, use half the amount of water. Wrap the remaining coconut block well and keep in the refrigerator for 3–4 weeks.

Caribbean Empanadas

Ingredients (Serves 4)

125 g/4oz lean fresh beef mince
125 g/4 oz lean fresh pork mince
1 onion, peeled and finely chopped
1 Scotch bonnet chilli, deseeded and finely chopped
1 small red pepper, deseeded and finely chopped
½ tsp ground cloves
1 tsp ground cinnamon
½ tsp ground allspice
1 tsp sugar
1 tbsp tomato purée
3–4 tbsp water
450 g/1 lb prepared shortcrust pastry
vegetable oil, for deep-frying
lime wedges to serve (optional)

Place all the mince in a nonstick frying pan and cook, stirring, for 5–8 minutes, or until sealed. Break up any lumps with a wooden spoon. Add the onion, chilli and red pepper together with the spices and cook, stirring, for 10 minutes, or until the onion has softened. Sprinkle in the sugar.

Blend the tomato purée with the water and stir into the meat. Bring to the boil, then reduce the heat and simmer for 10 minutes. Allow to cool.

Roll the pastry out on a lightly floured surface and cut into 10 cm/4 inch rounds. Place a spoonful of the meat mixture onto the centre of each pastry round and brush the edges with water. Fold over, encasing the filling to form small pasties.

Heat the oil to a temperature of 180°C/350°F and deep-fry the empanadas in batches, three or four at a time, for 3–4 minutes until golden. Drain on kitchen paper. Serve with lime wedes, if liked.

Tasty Tip

If preferred, the Empanadas can be oven baked. Brush witmelted butter then cook in a preheated oven at 200°C/400°F/Gas Mark 6 for 20 minutes.

Goan-style Beef Curry

Ingredients (Serves 4)

1 onion, peeled and chopped
2–3 garlic cloves, peeled and chopped
5 cm/2 inch piece fresh root ginger, peeled and grated
1 tsp chilli powder
1 tsp turmeric
1 tsp ground coriander
1 tsp ground cumin
freshly milled salt
450 g/1 lb stewing steak, trimmed
1 tbsp vegetable oil
1 green chilli, deseeded and cut in half lengthways
1 red chilli, deseeded and cut in half lengthways
450 ml/³/₄ pint beef stock

Place the onions, garlic, ginger and spices in a food processor and blend to a paste.

Spread half the paste half over the steak, then sprinkle lightly with salt. Leave to marinate in the refrigerator for at least 15 minutes.

Cut the beef into small strips. Heat 1 tablespoon of the oil in a heavy-based saucepan, add the beef and fry on all sides for 5 minutes, or until sealed. Remove from the pan and reserve.

Add the remaining oil to the pan, then add the halved chillies and fry for 2 minutes. Remove and reserve. Stir the remaining paste into the oil left in the pan and cook for a further 3 minutes. Return the beef to the pan with the beef stock and bring to the boil.

Reduce the heat, cover and simmer for 30–40 minutes until tender. Garnish with the halved chillies and serve.

Food Fact
Beef is not eaten in most parts of India as it is forbidden by the Hindu religion.

Cannelloni with Spicy Bolognese Filling

Ingredients (Serves 4)

8 dried cannelloni tubes
300 ml/¹/₂ pint prepared white sauce
25 g/1 oz freshly grated Parmesan cheese
¹/₄ tsp freshly grated nutmeg
crisp green salad, to serve

SPICY BOLOGNESE FILLING:
1 tbsp olive oil
1 small onion, peeled and finely chopped
2 garlic cloves, peeled and crushed
350 g/12 oz fresh lean beef mince
¹/₄ tsp crushed chilli flakes
2 tbsp freshly chopped oregano
400 g can whole peeled tomatoes, chopped
1 tbsp tomato purée
150 ml/¹/₄ pint beef stock
salt and freshly ground black pepper

 Preheat the oven to 200°C/400°F/Gas Mark 6, 15 minutes before cooking the stuffed cannelloni. For the filling,

heat the oil in a large heavy-based pan, add the onion and garlic and cook for 8 minutes, or until soft. Add the beef mince and cook, stirring with a wooden spoon to break up lumps, for 5–8 minutes, or until the meat is browned.

 Stir in the chilli flakes, oregano, tomatoes and tomato purée and pour in the stock. Season with salt and pepper. Bring to the boil, cover with a lid and lower the heat, then simmer for at least 30 minutes, stirring occasionally. Remove the lid and simmer for a further 10 minutes. Allow to cool slightly.

Using a teaspoon, fill the cannelloni tubes with the meat filling. Lay the stuffed cannelloni side by side in a lightly oiled ovenproof dish.

Pour the prepared white sauce over the cannelloni tubes and sprinkle with the Parmesan cheese and the nutmeg. Bake in the preheated oven for 30 minutes, or until golden brown and bubbling. Serve immediately with a green salad.

Tasty Tip

The bolognese filling can be made with just beef mince, as here, or more traditionally with a mixture of half beef and half lean pork mince. Minced chicken or turkey also work well in this recipe, although the colour is paler and the flavour less rich, but you can compensate for this by slightly increasing the quantity of herbs and spices.

Chilli Con Carne with Crispy-skinned Potatoes

Ingredients (Serves 4)

1 tbsp vegetable oil, plus extra for brushing
1 large onion, peeled and finely chopped
1 garlic clove, peeled and finely chopped
1 red chilli, deseeded and finely chopped
350 g/12 oz fresh lean beef mince
1 tbsp chilli powder
400 g can whole peeled tomatoes, chopped
2 tbsp tomato purée
400 g can red kidney beans, drained and rinsed
4 baking potatoes
coarse salt and freshly ground black pepper

TO SERVE:
ready-made guacamole (optional)
soured cream (optional)

Preheat the oven to 180°C/350°F/Gas Mark 4. Heat the oil in a large flameproof casserole dish and add the onion. Cook gently for 10 minutes until soft and lightly browned. Add the garlic and chilli and cook briefly. Increase the heat. Add the mince and cook for a further 10 minutes, stirring occasionally, until browned.

Add the chilli powder and stir well. Cook for about 2 minutes, then add the chopped tomatoes and tomato purée. Bring slowly to the boil. Cover and cook in the preheated oven for 1½ hours. Remove from the oven and stir in the kidney beans. Return to the oven for a further 15 minutes.

Meanwhile, brush a little vegetable oil all over the potatoes and rub on some coarse salt. Put the potatoes in the oven alongside the chilli.

Remove the chilli and potatoes from the oven. Cut a cross in each potato, then squeeze to open slightly and season to taste with salt and pepper. Serve with the chilli and, if using, the guacamole and soured cream.

Recipes:
Lamb

Braised Lamb with Broad Beans

Ingredients (Serves 4)

350 g/12 oz shoulder or neck of lamb, diced
1 tbsp plain flour
1 onion
2 garlic cloves
1 tbsp olive oil
400 g can whole peeled tomatoes, chopped
300 ml/½ pint lamb or chicken stock
2 tbsp freshly chopped oregano
salt and freshly ground black pepper
225 g/8 oz frozen broad beans
fresh oregano, to garnish
creamy mashed potatoes, to serve

 Trim the lamb, discarding any fat or gristle, then place the flour in a polythene bag, add the lamb and toss until coated thoroughly. Peel and slice the onion and garlic and reserve. Heat the olive oil in a heavy-based saucepan and, when hot, add the lamb and cook, stirring, until the meat is sealed and browned all over. Using a slotted spoon, transfer the lamb to a plate and reserve.

 Add the onion and garlic to the saucepan and cook for 3 minutes, stirring frequently until softened, then return the lamb to the saucepan. Add the chopped tomatoes with their juice, the stock and the chopped oregano and season to taste with salt and pepper. Bring to the boil, then cover with a close-fitting lid, reduce the heat and simmer for 1 hour.

 Add the broad beans to the lamb and simmer for 20–30 minutes until the lamb is tender. Garnish with fresh oregano and serve with creamy mashed potatoes.

Helpful Hint
When shopping, look for special offers – lamb can be quite expensive but is often on special offer. Look for diced boneless shoulder or neck, which are ideal for longer cooking.

Tagliatelle with Creamy Liver and Basil

Ingredients (Serves 4)

25 g/1 oz plain flour
salt and freshly ground black pepper
350 g/12 oz lamb's liver, thinly sliced and cut into bite-
    sized pieces
25 g/1 oz margarine or butter
1 tbsp olive oil
2 red onions, peeled and sliced
1 garlic clove, peeled and sliced
150 ml/¼ pint chicken stock
1 tbsp tomato purée
2 tomatoes, finely chopped
1 tbsp freshly chopped basil
150 ml/¼ pint single cream
350 g/12 oz tagliatelle verdi
fresh basil leaves, to garnish

 Season the flour lightly with salt and pepper and place in a large plastic bag. Add the liver and toss gently to coat. Remove the liver from the bag and reserve.

 Melt the margarine or butter with the olive oil in a large frying pan. Add the onion and garlic and fry for 6–8 minutes until the onions begin to colour. Add the liver and fry until brown on all sides.

Stir in the chicken stock, tomato purée and tomatoes. Bring to the boil, reduce the heat and simmer very gently for 10 minutes.

Meanwhile, bring a large pan of lightly salted water to a rolling boil. Add the pasta and cook according to the packet instructions, or until *al dente*.

Stir the chopped basil and cream into the liver sauce and season to taste.

Drain the pasta thoroughly, reserving 2 tablespoons of the cooking water. Tip the pasta into a warmed serving dish or pile on to individual plates. Stir the reserved cooking water into the liver sauce and pour over the pasta. Toss lightly to coat the pasta. Garnish with basil leaves and serve immediately.

Moroccan Lamb Pie with Apricots

Ingredients (Serves 4)

5 cm/2 inch piece root ginger, peeled and grated
3 garlic cloves, peeled and crushed
1 tsp ground cumin
1 tsp ground cinnamon
2 tbsp olive oil
350 g/12oz boneless shoulder or lamb neck fillet, cubed
1 large red onion, peeled and chopped
400 g can whole peeled tomatoes, chopped
50 g/2 oz ready-to-eat dried apricots
400 g can chickpeas, drained and rinsed
7 large sheets filo pastry
50 g/ 2 oz margarine or butter, melted
pinch nutmeg
dill sprigs, to garnish

 Preheat the oven to 190°C/375°F/Gas Mark 5. Pound the ginger, garlic, cumin and cinnamon to a paste with a pestle and mortar. Heat 1 tablespoon of the oil in a large frying pan and fry the paste for 3 minutes. Remove and reserve.

 Add the remaining oil and fry the lamb in batches for about 5 minutes until golden brown. Return all the lamb to the pan and add the onions and spice paste. Fry for 10 minutes, stirring occasionally.

 Add the tomatoes, cover and simmer for 15 minutes. Add the apricots and chickpeas and simmer for 15 minutes.

 Lightly oil a round 18 cm/7 inch springform cake tin. Lay one sheet of filo pastry in the base, allowing the excess to fall over the sides. Brush with margarine or butter, then layer five more sheets in the tin, brushing each with margarine or butter.

 Spoon in the filling, levelling the surface. Layer half the remaining filo sheets on top, again brushing each with margarine or butter. Fold the overhanging pastry over the top of the filling. Brush the remaining sheet with margarine or butter and scrunch up and place on top of the pie so that the whole pie is completely covered. Brush with melted margarine or butter once more.

 Bake in the preheated oven for 45 minutes, then remove and leave for 10 minutes. Unclip the tin and remove the pie. Sprinkle with the nutmeg, garnish with the dill sprigs and serve.

Risotto with Lambs' Kidneys and Caramelised Shallots

Ingredients (Serves 4)

8 lambs' kidneys, halved and cores removed
150 ml/¼ pint milk
2 tbsp olive oil
50 g/2 oz margarine or butter
275 g/10 oz shallots, peeled and halved if large
1 onion, peeled and finely chopped
2 garlic cloves, peeled and finely chopped
350 g/12 oz risotto rice
1.25 litres/2¼ pints chicken or vegetable
   stock, heated
1 tsp dried thyme
25 g/1 oz Parmesan cheese, grated
salt and freshly ground black pepper
fresh herbs, to garnish

 Place the lambs' kidneys in a bowl and pour the milk over. Leave to soak for 15–20 minutes, then drain and pat dry on absorbent kitchen paper. Discard the milk.

 Heat 1 tablespoon of the oil with 25 g/1 oz of the margarine or butter in a medium saucepan. Add the shallots, cover and cook for 10 minutes over a gentle heat. Remove the lid and cook for a further 10 minutes, or until tender and golden.

Meanwhile, heat the remaining oil with the remaining margarine or butter in a deep-sided frying pan. Add the onion and cook over a medium heat for 5–7 minutes until starting to brown. Add the garlic and cook briefly.

Stir in the rice and cook for a further minute until glossy and well coated in oil and margarine or butter. Add a ladleful or two of the stock and stir well until the stock is absorbed. Continue adding the stock, a ladleful at a time, and stirring well between additions, until all of the stock is added and the rice is just tender, but still firm. Remove from the heat.

 Meanwhile, when the rice is nearly cooked, increase the heat under the shallots. Add the thyme and kidneys. Cook for 3–4 minutes.

 Stir the cheese into the rice with the caramelised shallots and kidneys. Season to taste, garnish and serve.

Lamb with Black Cherry Sauce

Ingredients (Serves 4)

450 g/1 lb lamb fillet
2 tbsp light soy sauce
1 tsp Chinese five-spice powder
4 tbsp fresh orange juice
125 g/4 oz black cherry jam
150 ml/¼ pint stock
50 g/2 oz fresh black cherries
1 tbsp groundnut oil
1 tbsp freshly chopped coriander, to garnish

TO SERVE:
freshly cooked peas
freshly cooked noodles

Remove the skin and any fat from the lamb fillet and cut into thin slices. Place in a shallow dish. Mix together the soy sauce, Chinese five-spice powder and orange juice and pour over the meat. Cover and leave in the refrigerator for at least 30 minutes.

Meanwhile, blend the jam and the stock together, pour into a small saucepan and bring to the boil. Simmer gently for 10 minutes until slightly thickened. Remove the stones from the fresh cherries, using a cherry stoner if possible in order to keep them whole. Add the cherries to the sauce.

Drain the lamb when ready to cook. Heat the wok, add the oil and when the oil is hot, stir-fry the slices of lamb for 3–5 minutes until just slightly pink inside or cooked to personal preference.

Spoon the lamb into a warm serving dish and serve immediately with a little of the cherry sauce drizzled over. Garnish with the chopped coriander and the whole cherries and serve immediately with peas, freshly cooked noodles and the remaining sauce.

Moroccan Penne

Ingredients (Serves 4)

1 tbsp sunflower oil
1 red onion, peeled and chopped
2 cloves garlic, peeled and crushed
1 tbsp coriander seeds
$\frac{1}{4}$ tsp cumin seeds
$\frac{1}{4}$ tsp freshly grated nutmeg
450 g/1 lb lean fresh lamb mince
1 aubergine, trimmed and diced
400 g can whole peeled tomatoes, chopped
300 ml/$\frac{1}{2}$ pint vegetable stock
125 g/4 oz ready-to-eat apricots, chopped
12 black olives, pitted
salt and freshly ground black pepper
350 g/12 oz penne
1 tbsp toasted pine nuts, to garnish (optional)

Preheat the oven to 200°C/400°F/Gas Mark 6, 15 minutes before using. Heat the sunflower oil in a large flameproof casserole dish. Add the onion and fry for 5 minutes, or until softened.

Using a pestle and mortar, pound the garlic, coriander seeds, cumin seeds and grated nutmeg together into a paste. Add to the onion and cook for 3 minutes.

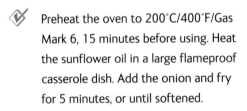

Add the lamb mince to the casserole dish and fry, stirring with a wooden spoon, for 4–5 minutes until the mince has broken up and browned.

Add the aubergine to the mince and fry for 5 minutes. Stir in the chopped tomatoes and vegetable stock and bring to the boil. Add the apricots and olives, then season well with salt and pepper. Return to the boil, lower the heat and simmer for 15 minutes.

Add the penne to the casserole dish, stir well, then cover and place in the preheated oven. Cook for 10 minutes, then stir and return to the oven, uncovered, for a further 15–20 minutes until the pasta is *al dente*. Remove from the oven, sprinkle with toasted pine nuts, if using, and serve immediately.

Lamb and Date Tagine

Ingredients (Serves 4)

few saffron strands
1 tbsp olive oil
1 onion, peeled and cut into wedges
2–3 garlic cloves, peeled and sliced
350 g/12 oz lamb, such as boneless shoulder or neck
  fillet, diced
1 cinnamon stick, bruised
1 tsp ground cumin
225 g/8 oz carrots, peeled and sliced
350 g/12 oz sweet potato, peeled and diced
900 ml/1½ pints lamb or vegetable stock
salt and freshly ground black pepper
125 g/4 oz dates, pitted and halved
freshly prepared couscous, to serve

Place the saffron in a small bowl, cover with warm water and leave to infuse for 10 minutes. Heat the oil in a large heavy-based pan, add the onion, garlic and lamb and sauté for 8–10 minutes until sealed. Add the cinnamon stick and ground cumin and cook, stirring constantly, for a further 2 minutes.

Add the carrots and sweet potato, then add the saffron with the soaking liquid and the stock. Bring to the boil, season to taste with salt and pepper, then reduce the heat to a simmer. Cover with a lid and simmer for 45 minutes, stirring occasionally.

Add the dates and continue to simmer for a further 15 minutes. Remove the cinnamon stick, adjust the seasoning and serve with freshly prepared couscous.

Helpful Hint
Replace the saffron with ½ tsp ground turmeric, add to the pan with the other spices.

Lamb Pilaf

Ingredients (Serves 4)

2 tbsp vegetable oil
25 g/1 oz flaked almonds
1 onion, peeled and finely chopped
1 carrot, peeled and finely chopped
1 celery stalk, trimmed and finely chopped
350 g/12 oz lamb, such as boneless shoulder or neck
    fillet, cut into chunks
$\frac{1}{4}$ tsp ground cinnamon
$\frac{1}{4}$-$\frac{1}{2}$ tsp crushed chilli flakes
2 large tomatoes, skinned, deseeded and chopped
grated zest of 1 orange
300 g/10 oz easy-cook brown basmati rice
600 ml/1 pint vegetable or lamb stock
2 tbsp freshly snipped chives
3 tbsp freshly chopped coriander
salt and freshly ground black pepper

TO GARNISH:
lemon slices
fresh coriander sprigs

Preheat the oven to 180°C/350°F/Gas Mark 4. Heat the oil in an ovenproof casserole with a tight-fitting lid and add the almonds. Fry for about 1 minute until just starting to brown, stirring often. Add the onion, carrot and celery and cook gently for a further 8–10 minutes until soft and lightly browned.

Increase the heat and add the lamb. Cook for a further 5 minutes until the lamb has changed colour. Add the ground cinnamon and chilli flakes and stir briefly before adding the tomatoes and orange zest.

Stir and add the rice, then the stock. Bring slowly to the boil and cover tightly. Transfer to the preheated oven and cook for 30–35 minutes until the rice is tender and the stock is absorbed.

Remove from the oven and leave to stand for 5 minutes before stirring in the chives and coriander. Season to taste with salt and pepper. Garnish with the lemon slices and fresh coriander sprigs and serve immediately.

Lamb Biryani

Ingredients (Serves 4-6)

250 g/9 oz basmati rice
4 tbsp vegetable oil
4 whole cloves
4 green cardamom pods, cracked
120 ml/4 fl oz natural yogurt
2 garlic cloves, peeled and crushed
small piece fresh root ginger, peeled and grated
1/2 tsp turmeric
2–3 tsp ground coriander
2 tsp ground cumin
350 g/12 oz boneless lean lamb, such as boneless
  shoulder, diced
2 onions, peeled and finely sliced
225 g/8 oz tomatoes, chopped
1 tbsp freshly chopped coriander
1 tbsp freshly chopped mint

 Rinse the rice at least two or three times then reserve. Heat 1 tablespoon of the oil in a saucepan, add the cloves and cardamom pods and fry for 30 seconds. Add the rice and cover with boiling water. Bring to the boil, reduce the heat, cover and simmer for 12–15 minutes until the rice is tender. Drain and reserve.

 Blend the yogurt, garlic, ginger, turmeric, ground coriander and cumin together with the lamb. Stir, cover and leave to marinate in the refrigerator for at least 2–3 hours.

 When ready to cook, preheat the oven to 200°C/400°F/Gas Mark 6. Heat the remaining oil in a large saucepan, add the onions and fry for 5 minutes, or until softened. Add the tomatoes. Using a slotted spoon, remove the lamb from the marinade, reserving the marinade, and add the lamb to the pan. Cook, stirring, for 5 minutes then add the remaining marinade. Cover and cook, stirring occasionally, for 25–30 minutes until the lamb is tender and the sauce is thick. Stir in the herbs.

 Oil an ovenproof dish. Spoon in a layer of rice and cover with a layer of lamb. Repeat, finishing with a layer of rice. Cover with foil and place in the oven for 10 minutes. Invert onto a warmed plate and serve.

Lamb Balti

Ingredients (Serves 4)

350 g/12 oz lamb, such as boneless shoulder or neck
    fillet, trimmed
2 tbsp vegetable oil
1–2 tbsp ready-made balti paste
2–3 garlic cloves, peeled and crushed
2–3 green chillies, deseeded and chopped
2 onions, peeled and chopped
1 aubergine, trimmed and chopped
4 tomatoes, chopped
2 tsp tomato purée
600 ml/1 pint lamb or vegetable stock
2 tbsp freshly chopped coriander
naan bread, to serve

Dice the lamb and reserve. Heat the oil in a large frying pan, add the balti paste and fry for 30 seconds.

Add the garlic, chillies, onions and aubergine. Cook, stirring, for a further 5 minutes, or until the vegetables are coated in the paste.

Add the lamb and continue to fry for 5–8 minutes until sealed. Stir in the chopped tomatoes. Blend the tomato purée with the stock, then pour into the pan. Bring to the boil, cover, reduce the heat and simmer for 45–50 minutes until the lamb is tender. Sprinkle with chopped coriander and serve with plenty of naan bread.

Food Fact
The Urdu pot that this is normally cooked in is known as a 'karahi'.

Lamb and Potato Curry

Ingredients (Serves 4)

350 g/12 oz boneless lamb, such as shoulder
2 tbsp vegetable oil
2 onions, peeled and cut into wedges
2–3 garlic cloves, peeled and sliced
2 celery stalks, trimmed and sliced
1–2 tbsp Madras curry powder
1 tbsp tomato purée
150 ml/¼ pint water
150 ml/¼ pint coconut milk
225 g/8 oz tomatoes, chopped
350 g/12 oz new potatoes, scrubbed
100 g/4 oz carrots, peeled and sliced

Discard any fat or gristle from the lamb, then cut into thin strips and reserve.

Heat the oil in a deep frying pan, add the onions, garlic and celery and fry for 5 minutes, or until softened. Add the curry powder and continue to fry for a further 2 minutes, stirring

constantly. Add the lamb and cook for 5 minutes, or until coated in the curry paste.

Blend the tomato purée with the water then stir into the pan together with the coconut milk and chopped tomatoes.

Cut the potatoes into small chunks and add to the pan with the carrots. Bring to the boil, then reduce the heat, cover and simmer for 25–30 minutes until the lamb and vegetables are tender.

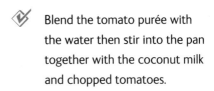

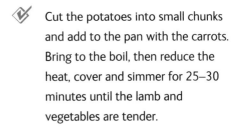

Recipes:
Poultry

Coriander Chicken and Soy Sauce Cakes

Ingredients (Serves 4)

¼ cucumber, peeled
1 shallot, peeled and thinly sliced
6 radishes, trimmed and sliced
350 g/12 oz skinless, boneless chicken thighs
4 tbsp roughly chopped fresh coriander
2 spring onions, trimmed and roughly chopped
2 red chillies, deseeded
finely grated zest of ½ lime
2 tbsp soy sauce
1 tbsp caster sugar
2 tbsp white wine or rice vinegar
1 red chilli, deseeded and finely sliced
freshly chopped coriander, to garnish

Preheat the oven to 190°C/375°F/Gas Mark 5. Halve the cucumber lengthways, deseed and dice.

In a bowl, mix the shallot and radishes. Chill until ready to serve with the diced cucumber.

Place the chicken thighs in a food processor and blend until coarsely chopped.

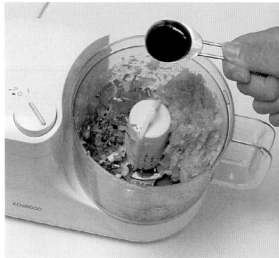

Add the coriander and spring onions to the chicken. Chop one of the chillies, then add to the food processor with the lime zest and soy sauce. Blend again until mixed.

Using slightly damp hands, shape the chicken mixture into 12 small rounds.

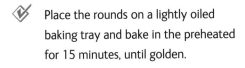 Place the rounds on a lightly oiled baking tray and bake in the preheated for 15 minutes, until golden.

In a small pan, heat the sugar with 2 tablespoons of water until dissolved. Simmer until syrupy.

Remove from the heat and allow to cool a little. Slice the remaining chilli then stir into the pan with the vinegar and chilli slices. Pour over the cucumber and the radish and shallot salad. Garnish with the chopped coriander and serve the chicken cakes with the salad immediately.

Tasty Tip

In this recipe, the chicken cakes can be altered so that half chicken and half lean pork is used. This alters the flavour of the dish and works really well if a small 2.5 cm/ 1 inch piece of fresh ginger is grated and added with the lime zest and soy sauce.

Chicken and Ham Pie

Ingredients (Serves 4)

1 tbsp olive oil
1 leek, trimmed and sliced
125g/4 oz piece of bacon, cut into small dice
225 g/8 oz cooked boneless chicken
salt and freshly ground black pepper
225 g/8 oz prepared shortcrust pastry
2 medium eggs, beaten
150 ml/¼ pint natural yogurt
4 tbsp chicken stock
1 tbsp poppy seeds

TO SERVE:
sliced red onion
mixed salad leaves

Preheat the oven to 200°C/400°F/Gas Mark 6. Heat the oil in a frying pan and fry the leek and bacon for 4 minutes until soft but not coloured. Transfer to a bowl and reserve.

Cut the chicken into bite-sized pieces and add to the leek and bacon. Season to taste with salt and pepper.

Roll out half the pastry on a lightly floured surface and use to line a 18 cm/7 inch loose-bottomed deep flan tin. Scoop the chicken mixture into the pastry case.

Mix together 1 egg, the yogurt and the chicken stock. Pour the yogurt mixture over the chicken. Roll out the remaining pastry on a lightly floured surface, and cut out the lid to 5 mm/ ¼ inch wider than the dish.

Brush the rim with the remaining beaten egg and lay the pastry lid on top, pressing the edges with the back of a knife to seal. Cut a hole in the centre to allow the steam to escape.

Sprinkle with the poppy seeds and bake in the preheated oven for about 30 minutes, or until the pastry is golden brown. Serve with the onion and mixed salad leaves.

Helpful Hint
Look for a gammon steak or bacon chop to use in this recipe.

Penne with Pan-fried Chicken and Capers

Ingredients (Serves 4)

350 g/12 oz boneless, skinless chicken thighs
25 g/1 oz plain flour
salt and freshly ground black pepper
350 g/12 oz penne
2 tbsp olive oil
1 red onion, peeled and sliced
1 garlic clove, peeled and chopped
2–4 tbsp pesto
200 g/7 oz cream cheese
1 tsp wholegrain mustard
1 tbsp lemon juice
2 tbsp freshly chopped basil
1 tbsp capers in brine, rinsed and drained
freshly shaved Pecorino Romano cheese

Trim the chicken and cut into bite-sized pieces. Season the flour with salt and pepper, then toss the chicken in the seasoned flour and reserve.

Bring a large saucepan of lightly salted water to a rolling boil. Add the penne and cook according to the packet instructions, or until *al dente*.

Meanwhile, heat the olive oil in a large frying pan. Add the chicken to the pan and cook for 8 minutes, or until golden on all sides, stirring frequently. Transfer the chicken to a plate and reserve.

Add the onion and garlic to the oil remaining in the frying pan and cook for 5 minutes, or until softened, stirring frequently.

Return the chicken to the frying pan. Stir in the pesto and cream cheese and heat through, stirring gently, until smooth. Stir in the wholegrain mustard, lemon juice, basil and capers. Season to taste, then continue to heat through until piping hot.

Drain the penne thoroughly and return to the saucepan. Pour over the sauce and toss well to coat. Arrange the pasta on individual warmed plates. Scatter with the cheese and serve immediately.

Spicy Mexican Chicken

2 tbsp olive oil
350 g/12 oz fresh chicken mince
1 red onion, peeled and chopped
2 garlic cloves, peeled and chopped
1 red pepper, deseeded and chopped
1–2 tsp hot chilli powder
2 tbsp tomato purée
225 ml/8 fl oz chicken stock
salt and freshly ground black pepper
200 g/7 oz can red kidney beans, drained
200 g/7 oz canned chilli beans, drained
350 g/12 oz spaghetti

TO SERVE (OPTIONAL):
Cheddar cheese, grated
guacamole
hot chilli salsa

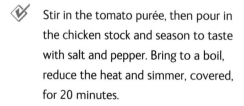 Heat the oil in a large frying pan, add the chicken mince and cook for 5 minutes, stirring frequently with a wooden spoon to break up any lumps. Add the onion, garlic and pepper and cook for 3 minutes. Stir in the chilli powder and cook for a further 2 minutes.

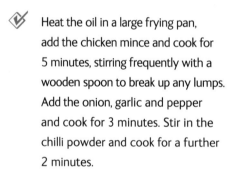 Stir in the tomato purée, then pour in the chicken stock and season to taste with salt and pepper. Bring to a boil, reduce the heat and simmer, covered, for 20 minutes.

Add the kidney and chilli beans and cook, stirring occasionally, for 10 minutes, or until the chicken is tender.

Meanwhile, bring a large pan of lightly salted water to a rolling boil. Add the spaghetti and cook according to the packet instructions, or until *al dente*.

Drain the spaghetti thoroughly, arrange on warmed plates and spoon over the chicken and bean mixture. Serve with the grated cheese, guacamole and salsa if using.

Helpful Hint
A range of chilli powders is available. The most usual is the red powder made from dried red chillies, which may be mild or hot. A darker powder, which contains a mixture of ground chilli and herbs, is specifically for use in Mexican and southwest American dishes.

Chicken Marengo

Ingredients (Serves 4)

2 tbsp plain flour
salt and freshly ground black pepper
4 boneless, skinless chicken thighs, cut into
    bite-sized pieces
3 tbsp olive oil
1 Spanish onion, peeled and chopped
1 garlic clove, peeled and chopped
400 g can whole peeled tomatoes, chopped
2 tbsp tomato purée
1 tbsp freshly chopped basil
1–2 tsp dried thyme
125 ml/4 fl oz chicken stock
350 g/12 oz rigatoni
3 tbsp freshly chopped flat-leaf parsley (optional)

 Season the flour with salt and pepper and toss the chicken in the flour to coat. Heat 2 tablespoons of the olive oil in a large frying pan and cook the chicken for 7 minutes, or until browned all over, turning occasionally. Remove from the pan, using a slotted spoon, and keep warm.

 Add the remaining oil to the pan, add the onion and cook, stirring occasionally, for 5 minutes, or until softened and starting to brown. Add the garlic, tomatoes, tomato purée, basil and thyme. Pour in the chicken stock and season well. Bring to the boil. Stir in the chicken pieces and simmer for 15 minutes, or until the chicken is tender and the sauce has thickened.

Meanwhile, bring a large pan of lightly salted water to a rolling boil. Add the rigatoni and cook according to the packet instructions, or until *al dente*.

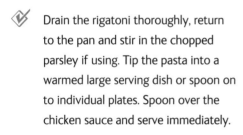 Drain the rigatoni thoroughly, return to the pan and stir in the chopped parsley if using. Tip the pasta into a warmed large serving dish or spoon on to individual plates. Spoon over the chicken sauce and serve immediately.

Helpful Hint

Spanish onions have a milder flavour and tend to be larger than English ones. Cook the onion over a fairly low heat until really soft, stirring frequently towards the end to stop it sticking. Let it caramelise and brown very slightly as this adds a richer flavour and golden colour to the final dish.

Spaghetti with Turkey and Bacon Sauce

Ingredients (Serves 4)

350 g/12 oz spaghetti
25 g/1 oz margarine or butter
125 g/4 oz smoked streaky bacon, rind removed
225 g/8 oz fresh turkey breast strips
1 onion, peeled and chopped
1 garlic clove, peeled and chopped
3 medium eggs, beaten
300 ml/½ pint single cream
salt and freshly ground black pepper
25 g/1 oz freshly grated Cheddar or Parmesan cheese
2–3 tbsp freshly chopped coriander, to garnish
  (optional)

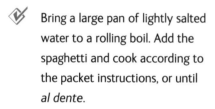

Bring a large pan of lightly salted water to a rolling boil. Add the spaghetti and cook according to the packet instructions, or until *al dente*.

Meanwhile, melt the margarine or butter in a large frying pan. Using a sharp knife, slice the streaky bacon finely. Add the bacon to the pan with the turkey strips and cook for 8 minutes, or until browned, stirring occasionally to prevent sticking. Add the onion and garlic and cook for 5 minutes, or until softened, stirring occasionally.

Place the eggs and cream in a bowl and season to taste with salt and pepper. Beat together, then pour into the frying pan and cook, stirring, for 2 minutes or until the mixture begins to thicken but does not scramble.

Drain the spaghetti thoroughly and return to the pan. Pour over the sauce, add the grated cheese and toss lightly. Heat through for 2 minutes, or until piping hot. Tip into a warmed serving dish and sprinkle with freshly chopped coriander, if using. Serve immediately.

Helpful Hint

It is a good idea to remove the pan from the heat before adding the beaten eggs to the pan, as there should be enough residual heat in the sauce to cook them. If the sauce does not start to thicken after 2 minutes, return to the heat and cook for 1–2 more minutes.

Turkey and Oven-Roasted Vegetable Salad

Ingredients (Serves 4)

4 tbsp olive oil
2 medium courgettes, trimmed and sliced
2 yellow peppers, deseeded and sliced
50 g/2 oz pine nuts
275 g/10 oz macaroni
350 g/12 oz cooked turkey
3 medium tomatoes, roughly chopped
2 tbsp freshly chopped coriander
1 garlic clove, peeled and chopped
3 tbsp balsamic vinegar
salt and freshly ground black pepper

Preheat the oven to 200°C/400°F/Gas Mark 6, 15 minutes before cooking. Line a large roasting tin with foil, pour in half the olive oil and place in the oven for 3 minutes, or until very hot. Remove from the oven, add the courgettes and peppers and stir until evenly coated. Bake for 30–35 minutes until slightly charred, turning occasionally.

Add the pine nuts to the tin. Return to the oven and cook for 10 minutes, or until the pine nuts are toasted. Remove from the oven and allow the vegetables to cool completely.

Bring a large pan of lightly salted water to a rolling boil. Add the macaroni and cook according to the packet instructions, or until *al dente*. Drain and refresh under cold running water then drain thoroughly and place in a large salad bowl.

Cut the turkey into bite-sized pieces and add to the macaroni. Add the tomatoes to the pan with the cooled vegetables and pan juices. Blend together the coriander, garlic, remaining oil, vinegar and seasoning. Pour over the salad, toss lightly and serve.

Mini Chicken Balls with Tagliatelle

Ingredients (Serves 4)

350 g/12 oz fresh chicken mince
25 g/1 oz sun-dried tomatoes, drained and finely
  chopped
salt and freshly ground black pepper
25 g/1 oz margarine or butter
1 tbsp vegetable oil
2 leeks, trimmed and diagonally sliced
125 g/4 oz frozen broad beans
300 ml/½ pint single cream
25 g/1 oz freshly grated Cheddar or Parmesan cheese
350 g/12 oz tagliatelle
4 medium eggs
fresh herbs, to garnish

Melt the margarine or butter in a large frying pan, add the chicken balls and cook for 5 minutes, or until golden, turning occasionally. Remove, drain on absorbent kitchen paper and keep warm.

Heat the oil in the pan, add the leeks and broad beans and cook, stirring, for 10 minutes or until cooked and tender. Return the chicken balls to the pan, then stir in the cream and cheese and heat through.

Mix the chicken mince and tomatoes together and season to taste with salt and pepper. Divide the mixture into 32 pieces and roll into balls. Transfer to a baking sheet, cover and leave in the refrigerator for 1 hour.

Meanwhile, bring a large pan of lightly salted water to a rolling boil. Add the pasta and cook according to the packet instructions, or until *al dente*.

Bring a separate frying pan full of water to the boil, crack in the eggs and simmer for 2–4 minutes, or until poached to personal preference.

Meanwhile, drain the pasta thoroughly and return to the pan. Pour the chicken balls and vegetable sauce over the pasta, toss lightly and heat through for 1–2 minutes. Arrange on warmed individual plates and top with the poached eggs. Garnish with fresh herbs and serve immediately.

Helpful Hint

Chilling the chicken balls firms them, so that they retain their shape when cooked. They need plenty of room for turning; if necessary cook in two batches, halving the margarine or butter for each. The margarine or butter must be sizzling before the meatballs are added.

Turkey and Mixed Mushroom Lasagne

Ingredients (Serves 4)

1 tbsp olive oil
225 g/8 oz mixed mushrooms, e.g. button,
   chestnut and portobello, wiped and sliced
15 g/½ oz margarine or butter
25 g/1 oz plain flour
300 ml/½ pint skimmed milk
1 bay leaf
225 g/8 oz cooked turkey, cubed
¼ tsp freshly grated nutmeg
salt and freshly ground black pepper
400 g can whole peeled tomatoes,
   drained and chopped
1 tsp dried mixed herbs
9 lasagne sheets (about 150 g/5 oz)
mixed salad leaves, to serve

FOR THE TOPPING:
200 ml/7 fl oz 0%-fat Greek yogurt
1 medium egg, lightly beaten
1 tbsp finely grated Parmesan cheese

Preheat the oven to 180°C/350°F/Gas Mark 4. Heat the oil and cook the mushrooms until tender and all the juices have evaporated. Remove and reserve.

Put the margarine or butter, flour, milk and bay leaf in the pan. Slowly bring to the boil, stirring until thickened. Simmer for 2–3 minutes. Remove the bay leaf and stir in the mushrooms, turkey, nutmeg, salt and pepper.

Mix together the tomatoes and mixed herbs and season with salt and pepper. Spoon half into the base of a 1.7 litre/3 pint ovenproof dish. Top with three sheets of lasagne, then with half the turkey mixture. Repeat the layers, then arrange the remaining three sheets of pasta on top.

Mix together the yogurt and egg. Spoon over the lasagne, spreading the mixture into the corners. Sprinkle with the grated cheese.

Cook in the preheated oven for 40–45 minutes until the top is golden brown and bubbly. Serve with a green salad.

Helpful Hint
Look for special offers on mushrooms. Uneven shapes and varying sizes are often sold at a reduced price.

Turkey and Tomato Tagine

Ingredients (Serves 4)

FOR THE MEATBALLS:
450 g/1 lb fresh turkey mince
1 small onion, peeled and very finely chopped
1 garlic clove, peeled and crushed
1 tbsp freshly chopped coriander
1 tsp ground cumin
1 tbsp olive oil
salt and freshly ground black pepper

FOR THE SAUCE:
1 onion, peeled and finely chopped
1 garlic clove, peeled and crushed
150 ml/¼ pint turkey stock
400 g can whole peeled tomatoes, chopped
½ tsp ground cumin
½ tsp ground cinnamon
pinch of cayenne pepper
freshly chopped parsley
freshly chopped herbs, to garnish
freshly cooked couscous or rice, to serve

Preheat the oven to 190°C/375°F/Gas Mark 5. Put all the ingredients for the meatballs, except the oil and salt and pepper, in a bowl, and mix well. Season to taste with salt and pepper. Shape into 20 balls, about the size of walnuts.

Put on a tray, cover lightly and chill in the refrigerator while making the sauce.

Put the onion and garlic in a pan with 125 ml/4 fl oz of the stock. Cook over a low heat until all the stock has evaporated. Continue cooking for 1 minute, or until the onions begin to colour.

Add the remaining stock to the pan with the tomatoes, cumin, cinnamon and cayenne pepper. Simmer for 10 minutes, until slightly thickened and reduced. Stir in the parsley and season to taste.

Heat the oil in a large nonstick frying pan and cook the meatballs in two batches until lightly browned all over.

Lift the meatballs out with a slotted spoon and drain on kitchen paper.

Pour the sauce into a tagine or an ovenproof casserole dish. Top with the meatballs, cover and cook in the preheated oven for 25–30 minutes, or until the meatballs are cooked through and the sauce is bubbling. Garnish with freshly chopped herbs and serve immediately on a bed of couscous or plain boiled rice.

Cheesy Chicken Burgers

Ingredients (Serves 4)

1 tbsp sunflower oil
1 small onion, peeled and finely chopped
1 garlic clove, peeled and crushed
½ red pepper, deseeded and finely chopped
350 g/12 oz fresh chicken mince
2 tbsp 0%-fat Greek yogurt
40 g/1½ oz fresh brown breadcrumbs
1 tbsp freshly chopped herbs, such as parsley
    or tarragon
50 g/2 oz Cheshire cheese, crumbled
salt and freshly ground black pepper

FOR THE SWEETCORN AND CARROT RELISH:
125g/4 oz cooked sweetcorn kernels, drained
1 small carrot, peeled and grated
½ green chilli, deseeded and finely chopped
2 tsp white wine vinegar
2 tsp light soft brown sugar

TO SERVE:
wholemeal or granary rolls
lettuce
sliced tomatoes
mixed salad leaves

Preheat the grill. Heat the oil in a frying pan and gently cook the onion and garlic for 5 minutes. Add the red pepper and cook for 5 minutes. Transfer into a mixing bowl and add the chicken, yogurt, breadcrumbs, herbs and cheese and season to taste with salt and pepper. Mix well.

Divide the mixture equally into six and shape into burgers. Cover and chill in the refrigerator for at least 20 minutes.

To make the relish, put all the ingredients in a small saucepan with 1 tablespoon of water and heat gently, stirring occasionally, until all the sugar has dissolved. Cover and cook over a low heat for 2 minutes, then uncover and cook for a further minute, or until the relish is thick.

Place the burgers on a lightly oiled grill pan and grill under a medium heat for 8–10 minutes on each side until browned and completely cooked through.

Warm the rolls if liked, then split in half and fill with the burgers, lettuce, sliced tomatoes and the prepared relish. Serve with mixed salad leaves.

Spiced Indian Roast Potatoes with Chicken

Ingredients (Serves 4)

450 g/1 lb waxy potatoes, peeled and cut into
  large chunks
salt and freshly ground black pepper
4 tbsp sunflower oil
8 small chicken drumsticks
1 Spanish onion, peeled and roughly chopped
2 large garlic cloves, peeled and crushed
1 red chilli
2 tsp fresh root ginger, peeled and finely grated
2 tsp ground cumin
2 tsp ground coriander
pinch of cayenne pepper
4 cardamom pods, crushed
fresh coriander sprigs, to garnish

 Preheat the oven to 190°C/375°F/Gas Mark 5, about 10 minutes before cooking. Parboil the potatoes for 5 minutes in lightly salted boiling water, then drain thoroughly and reserve. Heat the oil in a large frying pan, add the chicken drumsticks and cook until sealed on all sides. Remove and reserve.

 Add the onions to the pan and fry for 4–5 minutes until softened. Stir in the garlic, chilli and ginger and cook for 1 minute, stirring constantly. Stir in the ground cumin, coriander, cayenne pepper and crushed cardamom pods

and continue to cook, stirring, for a further minute.

 Add the potatoes to the pan, then add the chicken drumsticks. Season to taste with salt and pepper. Stir gently until the potatoes and chicken pieces are coated in the onion and spice mixture.

 Spoon into a large roasting tin and roast in the preheated oven for 35 minutes, or until the chicken and potatoes are cooked thoroughly. Garnish with fresh coriander and serve immediately.

Helpful Hint
Buy frozen chicken drumsticks as they are cheaper than fresh. Do make sure they are thoroughly thawed before cooking and do not re-freeze unless cooked through.

Chicken and Chickpea Korma

Ingredients (Serves 4)

350 g/12 oz skinless, boneless chicken, such as thighs
2 tbsp vegetable oil
2 onions, peeled and cut into wedges
2–4 garlic cloves, peeled and chopped
2–3 tbsp Korma curry paste
450 ml/¾ pint chicken stock
225 g/8 oz ripe tomatoes, peeled and chopped
400 g can chickpeas, drained and rinsed
4 tbsp single cream
6 spring onions, trimmed and diagonally sliced
Indian-style bread, to serve

Cut the chicken into small strips and reserve. Heat the oil in a wok or frying pan, add the chicken and cook, stirring, for 3 minutes, or until sealed. Remove and reserve.

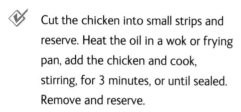

Add the onion and garlic to the pan and fry gently for 5 minutes, or until the onion has begun to soften. Add the curry paste and cook, stirring, for 2 minutes. Return the chicken to the pan and stir well.

Add the stock, tomatoes and chickpeas, then bring to the boil, reduce and simmer for 15–20 minutes until the chicken is cooked. Stir in the cream. Spoon into a warmed serving dish, sprinkle with the spring onions and serve with Indian-style bread.

Tasty Tip

This is a mild curry, so to make it hotter add either some fresh chillies or chilli powder. Remember to add with the garlic and curry paste.

Stir-fried Chinese Chicken Curry

Ingredients (Serves 4)

350 g/12 oz skinless, boneless chicken, such as thighs
1 egg white
1 tsp salt
1 tbsp cornflour
2 tbsp groundnut oil
225 g/8 oz carrots, peeled and cut into very
    thin batons
1 large red pepper, deseeded and cut into thin strips
1 large green pepper, deseeded and cut into thin strips
1–2 tbsp curry paste
175–200 ml/6–7 fl oz chicken stock
1 tbsp rice wine or white wine vinegar
1 tsp demerara sugar
1 tbsp light soy sauce
6 spring onions, trimmed and diagonally sliced
freshly cooked sticky rice, to serve

 Cut the chicken into small bite-sized pieces and place in a large bowl. Beat the egg white in a separate bowl until fluffy then beat in the salt and cornflour.

Pour over the chicken and leave to stand for 15 minutes. Heat a wok or frying pan and, when hot, add the oil. Heat for 30 seconds, then drain the chicken and add to the wok or frying pan and cook, stirring, for 2–3 minutes until sealed.

Remove the chicken and reserve. Add the carrots and peppers to the wok or frying pan and cook, stirring, for 3 minutes, or until the carrots have begun to soften. Stir in the curry paste and cook, stirring, for a further 2 minutes.

Add the stock, rice wine or vinegar, sugar and soy sauce. Stir well until blended then return the chicken to the pan with the spring onions. Cook for 3–4 minutes until the chicken is thoroughly cooked. Serve with the sticky rice.

Helpful Hint
Marinating the chicken in the egg white and salt helps to tenderise the chicken before cooking.

Hot Chicken Drumsticks

Ingredients (Serves 4)

4-8 chicken drumsticks, depending on size
2 tbsp vegetable oil
1 tsp fennel seeds
4 garlic cloves, peeled and chopped
1 onion, peeled and chopped
5 cm/2 inch piece fresh root ginger, peeled and grated
1 tsp ground coriander
1 tsp chilli powder
1–2 tsp curry powder
1 tbsp hot pepper sauce, or to taste
400 g can whole peeled tomatoes, chopped
200 ml/7 fl oz chicken stock
2 tbsp fresh thyme leaves
225 g/8 oz fresh spinach, chopped
freshly cooked new potatoes, to serve

 Discard the skin from the drumsticks, if preferred, and lightly rinse, then pat dry on absorbent kitchen paper. Heat the oil in a large frying pan, add the fennel seeds and cook for 30 seconds, or until they pop. Add the garlic, onion, ginger, ground coriander, chilli and curry powder and cook gently for 10 minutes, stirring frequently.

 Push the onion mixture to the side of the pan and add the chicken. Fry the chicken until it is browned on all sides.

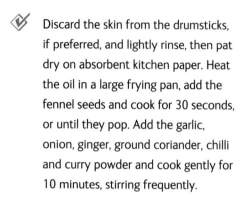 Add the hot pepper sauce to taste and the chopped tomatoes. Stir in the stock and thyme leaves. Bring to the boil, then reduce the heat, cover and simmer for 20–25 minutes until the chicken is cooked. Stir in the chopped spinach and heat for a further 3–4 minutes until the spinach has wilted. Serve with new potatoes.

Tasty Tip

The hot pepper sauce could be replaced with Tabasco sauce, which is also seriously hot. For those who prefer a slightly milder taste, use sweet chilli sauce.

Bengali Chicken Curry

Ingredients (Serves 4)

2–3 red chillies, deseeded and chopped
3 garlic cloves, peeled and chopped
5 cm/2 inch piece root ginger, peeled and grated
4 shallots, peeled and chopped
1 tsp turmeric
1–2 tsp curry powder
250 ml/8 fl oz water
350 g/12 oz skinless, boneless chicken, such as thighs
2 tbsp vegetable oil
1 tbsp freshly chopped coriander

TO SERVE:
Indian-style bread
salad

 Place the chillies, garlic, ginger, shallots, turmeric, curry powder and 150 ml/¼ pint of the water in a food processor until smooth, then reserve until required.

 Lightly rinse the chicken and pat dry with absorbent kitchen paper. Cut the chicken into thin strips, then place in a shallow dish and pour over the spice mixture. Cover and leave to marinate in the refrigerator for 15–30 minutes, stirring occasionally.

 Heat 2 tablespoons of the oil in a heavy-based frying pan then, using a slotted spoon, remove the chicken from the marinade, reserving the marinade. Cook the chicken for 10 minutes, or until sealed.

 Remove the chicken and reserve. Pour the reserved marinade into the pan and cook gently for 2 minutes. Return the chicken to the pan together with the remaining water. Bring to the boil, then reduce the heat and simmer for 15 minutes, stirring occasionally, until the chicken is cooked. Spoon into a warmed serving dish, sprinkle with the chopped coriander and serve with bread and salad.

Tasty Tip
This recipe works well with other meats as well as vegetables. If using other meat, ensure that it is thoroughly cooked before serving.

North Indian Slow-cooked Chicken

Ingredients (Serves 4)

8 small chicken thighs
3-4 tbsp vegetable oil
2 onions, peeled and cut into wedges
2–3 garlic cloves, peeled and sliced
1 green chilli, deseeded and sliced
1 red chilli, deseeded and sliced
2–3 tbsp Madras curry paste, or to taste
450 ml/³⁄₄ pint water
2 tbsp lemon juice
2 tbsp sesame seeds
fresh coriander sprigs, to garnish
freshly cooked rice, to serve

 Lightly rinse the chicken and pat dry with absorbent kitchen paper. Heat 2 tablespoons of the oil in a large deep frying pan, add the chicken and brown on all sides. Remove and reserve.

Add a further tablespoon of oil, if necessary, to the pan then add the onions, garlic and half the chillies and fry for 5 minutes, or until beginning to soften. Stir in the curry paste and cook for 2 minutes, stirring frequently. Take care not to burn the mixture.

Take off the heat, return the chicken to the pan and roll around in the paste until lightly coated. Stir in the water. Return to the heat and bring to the boil. Reduce the heat, cover and simmer for 35 minutes, or until the chicken is tender. Pour the lemon juice over the chicken and cook for a further 10 minutes.

Meanwhile, heat the remaining oil in a small frying pan and gently fry the rest of the chillies and the sesame seeds until the chillies have become crisp and the seeds are toasted. Serve the chicken on a bed of rice, sprinkled with the crispy chillies and toasted sesame seeds and garnished with coriander sprigs.

Helpful Hint
Use a chilli that has a heat tolerance between 3 and 5.

Sweet and Sour Rice with Chicken

Ingredients (Serves 4)

4 spring onions
2 tsp olive oil
1 tsp Chinese five-spice powder
350 g/12 oz skinless chicken thighs or breast fillets
1 tbsp vegetable oil
1 garlic clove, peeled and crushed
1 onion, peeled and sliced into thin wedges
225 g/8 oz white basmati rice
600 ml/1 pint water
4 tbsp tomato ketchup
1 tbsp tomato purée
2 tbsp honey
1 tbsp vinegar
1 tbsp dark soy sauce
1 carrot, peeled and cut into matchsticks

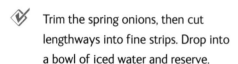

Trim the spring onions, then cut lengthways into fine strips. Drop into a bowl of iced water and reserve.

Mix together the olive oil and Chinese five-spice powder and use to rub into the chicken, then cut into small pieces. Heat the wok, then add the vegetable oil and, when hot, cook the garlic and onion for 2–3 minutes until transparent and softened.

Add the chicken to the wok and stir-fry over a medium-high heat until the chicken is golden and cooked through. Using a slotted spoon, remove from the wok and keep warm.

Stir the rice into the wok and add the water, tomato ketchup, tomato purée, honey, vinegar, soy sauce and carrot. Return the chicken to the wok and stir. Bring to the boil, then simmer for 15 minutes or until almost all of the liquid is absorbed. Spoon into a warmed dish. Drain the spring onions and place on top, then serve immediately.

Food Fact
Five-spice powder is a mixture of finely ground star anise, fennel, cinnamon, cloves and Szechuan pepper and adds a unique sweet and spicy aniseed flavour to food.

Turkey Hash with Potato and Beetroot

Ingredients (Serves 4)

2 tbsp vegetable oil
50 g/2 oz margarine or butter
4 slices streaky bacon, rind and cartilage removed,
    then diced or sliced
1 onion, peeled and finely chopped
350 g/12oz cooked turkey meat, diced
450 g/1 lb cooked potatoes, sliced
2–3 tbsp freshly chopped parsley
2 tbsp plain flour
250 g/9 oz (plain) cooked beetroot, diced
green salad, to serve

In a large heavy-based frying pan, heat the oil and half the margarine or butter over a medium heat until sizzling. Add the bacon and cook for 4 minutes, or until crisp and golden, stirring occasionally. Using a slotted

spoon, transfer to a large bowl. Add the onion to the pan and cook for 5-8 minutes until soft and golden, stirring frequently.

Meanwhile, add the turkey, potatoes, parsley and flour to the cooked bacon in the bowl. Stir and toss gently, then fold in the diced beetroot.

Add half the remaining margarine or butter to the frying pan and then the turkey-vegetable mixture. Stir, then spread the mixture to cover the bottom of the frying pan evenly. Cook for 15 minutes, or until the underside is crisp and brown, pressing the hash firmly into a cake with a spatula. Remove from the heat.

Invert a large plate over the frying pan and, holding the plate and frying pan together with an oven glove, turn the hash out onto the plate. Heat the remaining margarine or butter in the pan, slide the hash back into the pan and cook for 4 minutes, or until crisp and brown on the other side. Invert onto the plate again and serve immediately with a green salad.

Turkey Chow Mein

Ingredients (Serves 4)

225 g/8 oz fine egg noodles
2–3 tbsp sunflower oil
4 tsp light soy sauce
2 tbsp Chinese rice wine or white wine vinegar
salt and freshly ground black pepper
225 g/8 oz turkey steak, cut into strips
2 garlic cloves, peeled and finely chopped
50 g/2 oz mangetout, finely sliced
50 g/2 oz cooked ham, cut into fine strips
2 tsp dark soy sauce
pinch sugar

TO GARNISH:
shredded spring onions
toasted sesame seeds (optional)

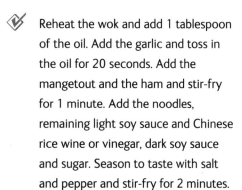

Place the egg noodles in a large bowl and cover with boiling water. Leave for 3–5 minutes, drain and add 1 tablespoon of the oil and stir lightly. Reserve.

Place 2 teaspoons of the light soy sauce, 1 tablespoon of the Chinese rice wine or vinegar and 1 teaspoon of the oil with seasoning to taste in a bowl. Add the turkey and stir well. Cover lightly and leave to marinate in the refrigerator for about 15 minutes.

Heat the wok over a high heat, add 1 tablespoon of oil and, when very hot, add the turkey and its marinade and stir-fry for 2 minutes. Remove the turkey and juices and reserve. Wipe the wok clean with absorbent kitchen paper.

Reheat the wok and add 1 tablespoon of the oil. Add the garlic and toss in the oil for 20 seconds. Add the mangetout and the ham and stir-fry for 1 minute. Add the noodles, remaining light soy sauce and Chinese rice wine or vinegar, dark soy sauce and sugar. Season to taste with salt and pepper and stir-fry for 2 minutes.

Add the turkey and juices to the wok and stir-fry for 4 minutes, or until the turkey is cooked. Garnish with spring onions and sesame seeds, if using, and serve.

Thai Chicken Fried Rice

Ingredients (Serves 4)

175 g/6 oz chicken breast fillets
2 tbsp vegetable oil
2 garlic cloves, peeled and
   finely chopped
2-3 tsp Thai red curry paste, or to taste
450 g/1 lb cold cooked rice
1 tbsp light soy sauce
2 tbsp Thai fish sauce
large pinch sugar
freshly ground black pepper

TO GARNISH:
2 spring onions, trimmed and shredded lengthways
½ small onion, peeled and very
   finely sliced

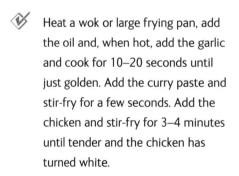

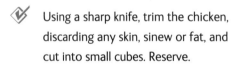

Using a sharp knife, trim the chicken, discarding any skin, sinew or fat, and cut into small cubes. Reserve.

Heat a wok or large frying pan, add the oil and, when hot, add the garlic and cook for 10–20 seconds until just golden. Add the curry paste and stir-fry for a few seconds. Add the chicken and stir-fry for 3–4 minutes until tender and the chicken has turned white.

Stir the cold cooked rice into the chicken mixture, then add the soy sauce, fish sauce and sugar, stirring well after each addition. Cook, stirring, for 5-8 minutes, or until the chicken is cooked through and the rice is piping hot.

Check the seasoning and, if necessary, add a little extra soy sauce. Turn the rice and chicken mixture into a warmed serving dish. Season lightly with black pepper and garnish with shredded spring onion and onion slices. Serve immediately.

Helpful Hint
Store cooked rice in a refrigerator overnight in a bowl with a tight-fitting lid or clingfilm.

Recipes:
Vegetables &
Vegetarian

Parsnip Tatin

Ingredients (Serves 4)

1 quantity prepared shortcrust pastry (*see* page 80 –
or about 175 g/6 oz ready-made)

FOR THE FILLING:
50 g/2 oz margarine or butter
8 small parsnips, peeled and halved
1 tbsp brown sugar
75 ml/3 fl oz apple juice

Preheat the oven to 200°C/400°F/Gas Mark 6. Heat the margarine or butter in a 20 cm/8 inch frying pan.

Add the parsnips, arranging the cut side down with the narrow ends towards the centre.

Sprinkle the parsnips with sugar and cook for 15 minutes, turning halfway through, until golden.

Add the apple juice and bring to the boil. Remove the pan from the heat.

On a lightly floured surface, roll the pastry out to a size slightly larger than the frying pan.

Position the pastry over the parsnips and press down slightly to enclose the parsnips.

Bake in the preheated oven for 20–25 minutes until the parsnips and pastry are golden.

Invert a warm serving plate over the pan and carefully turn the pan over to flip the tart on to the plate. Serve immediately.

Helpful Hint

Serve this tart with freshly cooked mixed vegetables, such as carrots, leeks and sweetcorn, sprinkled with grated cheese for a substantial meal.

Spinach, Pine Nut and Mascarpone Pizza

Ingredients (Serves 4)

1 quantity pizza dough (see page 130)

FOR THE TOPPING:
3 tbsp olive oil
1 large red onion, peeled and chopped
2 garlic cloves, peeled and finely sliced
450 g/1 lb frozen spinach, thawed and drained
salt and freshly ground black pepper
3 tbsp tomato purée
125 g/4 oz mascarpone cheese
1 tbsp toasted pine nuts

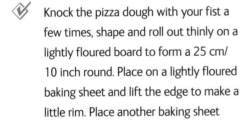 Knock the pizza dough with your fist a few times, shape and roll out thinly on a lightly floured board to form a 25 cm/ 10 inch round. Place on a lightly floured baking sheet and lift the edge to make a little rim. Place another baking sheet into the preheated oven to heat up.

Heat half the oil in a frying pan and gently fry the onion and garlic until soft and starting to change colour.

Squeeze out any excess water from the spinach and finely chop. Add to the onion and garlic with the remaining olive oil. Season to taste with salt and pepper.

Spread the tomato purée on the pizza dough and top with the spinach mixture. Mix the mascarpone with the pine nuts and dot over the pizza.

Slide the pizza on to the hot baking sheet and bake for 15–20 minutes. Transfer to a large plate and serve immediately.

Food Fact
Traditionally, mozzarella cheese is used for pizza topping, but this recipe incorporates another Italian cheese – mascarpone – which gives a creamy textured result to complement the delicate spinach and pine nut topping.

Stuffed Vine Leaves

Ingredients (Serves 4)

125 g/4 oz long-grain rice
125 g/4 oz fresh or preserved vine leaves
125 g/4 oz red onion, peeled and finely chopped
2 baby leeks, trimmed and finely sliced
2 tbsp freshly chopped parsley
2 tbsp freshly chopped mint
2 tbsp freshly chopped dill
125 ml/4 fl oz olive oil
salt and freshly ground black pepper
40 g/1½ oz currants
40 g/1½ oz ready-to-eat dried apricots,
   finely chopped
2 tbsp pine nuts
juice of 1 lemon
600 ml/1 pint boiling stock
lemon wedges or slices, to garnish
4 tbsp Greek-style yogurt, to serve

drain. If using preserved vine leaves, soak in tepid water for at least 20 minutes, drain, rinse and pat dry with absorbent kitchen paper.

 Mix the onion and leeks with the herbs and half the oil. Add the drained rice, mix and season to taste with salt and pepper. Stir in the currants, apricots, pine nuts and lemon juice. Spoon 1 teaspoon of the filling at the stalk end of each leaf. Roll, tucking the

Soak the rice in cold water for 30 minutes. If using fresh vine leaves, blanch 5–6 leaves at a time in salted boiling water for a minute. Rinse and

side flaps into the centre to create a neat parcel; do not roll too tight. Continue until all the filling is used.

Layer half the remaining vine leaves over the base of a large frying pan. Pack the little parcels in the frying pan and cover with the remaining leaves.

Pour in enough stock to just cover the vine leaves, add a pinch of salt and bring to the boil. Reduce the heat, cover and simmer for 45–55 minutes until the rice is sticky and tender. Leave to stand for 10 minutes. Drain the stock. Garnish with lemon wedges and serve hot with the Greek yogurt.

Helpful Hint

Use blanched cabbage leaves or iceberg lettuce leaves in place of the vine leaves.

Beetroot Risotto

Ingredients (Serves 4)

4 tbsp olive oil
1 onion, peeled and finely chopped
2 garlic cloves, peeled and finely chopped
2 tsp freshly chopped thyme
1 tsp grated lemon zest
300 g/10 oz risotto rice
750–900 ml/1¼–1½ pints vegetable stock, heated
2 tbsp single cream (optional)
225 g/8 oz cooked beetroot, peeled and
    finely chopped
2 tbsp freshly chopped parsley
25 g/1 oz Parmesan cheese, freshly grated
salt and freshly ground black pepper
sprigs of fresh thyme, to garnish

Heat half the oil in a large heavy-based frying pan. Add the onion, garlic, thyme and lemon zest. Cook for 5 minutes, stirring frequently, until the onion is soft and transparent but not coloured. Add the rice and stir until it is well coated in the oil.

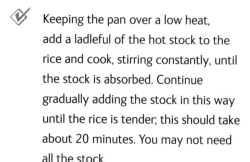

Keeping the pan over a low heat, add a ladleful of the hot stock to the rice and cook, stirring constantly, until the stock is absorbed. Continue gradually adding the stock in this way until the rice is tender; this should take about 20 minutes. You may not need all the stock.

Stir in the cream, if using, chopped beetroot, parsley and half the grated Parmesan cheese. Season to taste with salt and pepper. Garnish with sprigs of fresh thyme and serve immediately with the remaining grated Parmesan cheese.

Tasty Tip

If you buy ready-cooked beetroot, choose small ones, which are sweeter. Make sure that they are not doused in vinegar as this would spoil the flavour of the dish. If cooking your own, try baking them instead of boiling. Leave the stems intact and gently scrub to remove any dirt. Put them in a baking dish, cover loosely with foil and cook in a preheated oven at 170°C/325°F/ Gas Mark 3 for 2 hours. Once cool enough to handle, the skins should slip off.

Tomato and Courgette Herb Tart

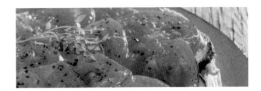

Ingredients (Serves 4)

4 tbsp olive oil
1 onion, peeled and finely chopped
3 garlic cloves, peeled and crushed
400 g/14 oz prepared puff pastry, thawed if frozen
1 small egg, beaten
2 tbsp freshly chopped rosemary
2 tbsp freshly chopped parsley
175 g/6 oz rindless fresh soft goats' cheese
4 ripe plum tomatoes, sliced
1 medium courgette, trimmed and sliced
thyme sprigs, to garnish

Preheat the oven to 230°C/450°F/Gas Mark 8. Heat 2 tablespoons of the oil in a large frying pan.

Fry the onion and garlic for about 4 minutes until softened and reserve.

Roll out the pastry on a lightly floured surface, and cut out a 30 cm/12 inch circle.

Brush the pastry with a little beaten egg, then prick all over with a fork.

Transfer on to a dampened baking sheet and bake in the preheated oven for 10 minutes.

Turn the pastry over and brush with a little more egg. Bake for 5 more minutes, then remove from the oven.

Mix together the onion, garlic and herbs with the goats' cheese and spread over the pastry.

Arrange the tomatoes and courgettes over the goats' cheese and drizzle with the remaining oil.

Bake for 20–25 minutes until the pastry is golden brown and the topping bubbling. Garnish with the thyme sprigs and serve immediately.

Tasty Tip

Goats' cheese works particularly well in this recipe, complementing both the tomato and courgette. Be aware though that it can tend to be a little acidic, so it is best to try to choose a creamy variety, which will mellow even more once baked.

Three Tomato Pizza

Ingredients (Serves 4)

1 quantity pizza dough (see page 201)
3 plum tomatoes
8 cherry tomatoes
6 sun-dried tomatoes
pinch sea salt
1 tbsp freshly chopped basil
2 tbsp olive oil
125 g/4 oz buffalo mozzarella cheese, sliced
freshly ground black pepper
fresh basil leaves, to garnish

Preheat the oven to 220°C/425°F/Gas Mark 7. Place a baking sheet into the oven to heat up.

Divide the prepared pizza dough into four equal pieces.

Roll out one quarter of the pizza dough on a lightly floured board to form a 20 cm/8 inch round.

Meanwhile, lightly cover the three remaining pieces of dough with clingfilm.

Roll out the other three pieces into rounds, one at a time. While rolling out any piece of dough, keep the others covered with clingfilm.

Slice the plum tomatoes, halve the cherry tomatoes and chop the sun-dried tomatoes into small pieces.

Place a few pieces of each type of tomato on each pizza base then season to taste with the sea salt.

Sprinkle with the chopped basil and drizzle with the olive oil. Place a few slices of mozzarella on each pizza and season with black pepper.

Transfer the pizza on to the heated baking sheet and cook for 15–20 minutes until the cheese is golden brown and bubbling. Garnish with the basil leaves and serve immediately.

Helpful Hint
This recipe works very well if simply using fresh sliced tomatoes.

Roasted Vegetable Pie

Ingredients (Serves 4)

225 g/8 oz plain flour
pinch of salt
50 g/2 oz white vegetable fat cut into squares
50 g/2 oz margarine or butter, cut into squares
2 tsp herbes de Provence
1 red pepper, deseeded and halved
1 green pepper, deseeded and halved
1 yellow pepper, deseeded and halved
3 tbsp olive oil
1 aubergine, trimmed and sliced
1 courgette, trimmed and halved lengthways
1 leek, trimmed and cut into chunks
1 medium egg, beaten
125 g/4 oz mozzarella cheese, sliced
salt and freshly ground black pepper
mixed herb sprigs, to garnish

 Preheat the oven to 220°C/425°F/Gas Mark 7. Sift the flour and salt into a large bowl, add the fats and mix lightly. Using the fingertips, rub until the mixture resembles breadcrumbs. Stir in the herbs. Sprinkle over 1 tablespoon cold water and, with a knife, start bringing the dough together. (It may be necessary to use the hands for the final stage.) If the dough does not form a ball instantly, add a little more water. Place in a polythene bag and chill for 30 minutes.

 Place the peppers on a baking tray and sprinkle with 1 tablespoon oil. Brush the aubergines, courgettes and leeks with oil and add to the peppers. Roast in the oven for 20 minutes. Place the blackened peppers in a polythene bag and leave for 5 minutes. When cool enough to handle, peel the skins off.

 Roll out half the pastry on a lightly floured surface and use to line a 20 cm/8 inch round pie dish. Line the pastry with greaseproof paper, fill with baking beans or rice and bake blind for about 10 minutes. Remove the beans and the paper, then brush the base with a little of the beaten egg. Return to the oven for 5 minutes.

Layer the cooked vegetables and the cheese in the pastry case, seasoning each layer. Roll out the remaining pastry on a lightly floured surface, and cut out the lid 5 mm/¼ inch wider than the dish. Brush the rim with the beaten egg and lay the pastry lid on top, press to seal. Knock the edges with the back of a knife. Cut a slit in the lid and brush with the beaten egg. Bake for 30 minutes. Transfer to a large serving dish, garnish with sprigs of mixed herbs and serve immediately.

Vegetarian Spaghetti Bolognese

Ingredients (Serves 4)

2 tbsp olive oil
1 onion, peeled and finely chopped
1 carrot, peeled and finely chopped
1 celery stalk, trimmed and finely chopped
225 g/8 oz Quorn mince
450 ml/³⁄₄ pint vegetable stock
1 tsp mushroom ketchup (optional)
4 tbsp tomato purée
350 g/12 oz dried spaghetti
4 tbsp half-fat crème fraîche
salt and freshly ground black pepper
1 tbsp freshly chopped parsley

Add the Quorn mince and cook, stirring, for a further 2–3 minutes.

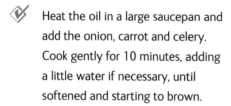

Heat the oil in a large saucepan and add the onion, carrot and celery. Cook gently for 10 minutes, adding a little water if necessary, until softened and starting to brown.

Mix together the vegetable stock and mushroom ketchup, if using, and add about half to the Quorn mixture along with the tomato purée. Cover and simmer gently for about 45 minutes, adding the remaining stock as necessary.

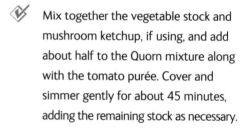

Meanwhile, bring a large pan of salted water to the boil and add the spaghetti. Cook until *al dente* or according to the packet instructions. Drain well. Remove the sauce from the heat, add the crème fraîche and season to taste with salt and pepper. Stir in the parsley and serve immediately with the pasta.

Helpful Hint

If liked, replace the mushroom ketchup with 50 g/2 oz chopped mushrooms. Add to pan with the Quorn. Instead of Quorn, an equivalent amount of soya mince can be used in this recipe, whether dried (follow the packet instructions) or frozen.

Potato and Goats' Cheese Tart

Ingredients (Serves 6)

275 g/10 oz prepared shortcrust pastry,
   thawed if frozen
550 g/1¼ lb small waxy potatoes
salt and freshly ground black pepper
beaten egg, for brushing
2 tbsp tomato purée
¼ tsp chilli powder, or to taste
1 large egg
150 ml/¼ pint soured cream
150 ml/¼ pint milk
2 tbsp freshly snipped chives
250 g/9 oz goats' cheese, sliced
salad and warm crusty bread, to serve

Preheat the oven to 190°C/375°F/Gas Mark 5, about 10 minutes before cooking. Roll the pastry out on a lightly floured surface and use to line a 23 cm/9 inch fluted flan tin. Chill in the refrigerator for 30 minutes.

Scrub the potatoes, place in a large saucepan of lightly salted water and bring to the boil. Simmer for 10–15 minutes until the potatoes are tender. Drain and reserve until cool enough to handle.

Line the pastry case with greaseproof paper and baking beans or crumpled foil and bake blind in the preheated oven for 15 minutes. Remove from the oven and discard the paper and beans or foil. Brush the base with a little beaten egg, then return to the oven and cook for a further 5 minutes. Remove from the oven.

Cut the potatoes into 1 cm/½ inch thick slices; reserve. Spread the tomato purée over the base of pastry case, sprinkle with the chilli powder, then arrange the potato slices on top in a decorative pattern.

Beat together the egg, soured cream, milk and chives, then season to taste with salt and pepper. Pour over the potatoes. Arrange the goats' cheese on top of the potatoes. Bake in the preheated oven for 30 minutes until golden brown and set. Serve immediately with salad and warm bread.

Warm Potato, Pear and Pecan Salad

Ingredients (Serves 4)

550 g/1¼ lb new potatoes, preferably
    red-skinned, unpeeled
salt and freshly ground black pepper
1 tsp Dijon mustard
2 tsp white wine vinegar
3 tbsp groundnut oil
1 tbsp hazelnut or walnut oil
2 tsp poppy seeds
2 firm ripe dessert pears
2 tsp lemon juice
175 g/6 oz baby spinach leaves
75 g/3 oz toasted pecan nuts

Scrub the potatoes, then cook in a saucepan of lightly salted boiling water for 15 minutes, or until tender. Drain, cut into halves, or quarters if large, and place in a serving bowl.

In a small bowl or jug, whisk together the mustard and vinegar. Gradually add the oils until the mixture begins to thicken. Stir in the poppy seeds and season to taste with salt and pepper.

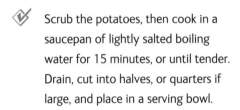

Pour about two thirds of the dressing over the hot potatoes and toss gently to coat. Leave until the potatoes have soaked up the dressing and are just warm.

Meanwhile, quarter and core the pears. Cut into thin slices, then sprinkle with the lemon juice to prevent them from going brown. Add to the potatoes with the spinach leaves and toasted pecan nuts. Gently mix together.

Drizzle the remaining dressing over the salad. Serve immediately before the spinach starts to wilt.

Helpful Hint

To toast the pecan nuts, place on a baking tray in a single layer and cook in a preheated oven at 180°C/350°F/Gas Mark 4 for 5 minutes, or under a medium grill for 3–4 minutes, turning frequently. Watch them carefully – they burn easily. If you cannot get red-skinned new potatoes for this dish, add colour by using red-skinned pears instead. Look out for Red Bartlett or Red Williams.

Aduki Bean and Rice Burgers

Ingredients (Serves 4)

2½ tbsp sunflower oil
1 medium onion, peeled and very finely chopped
1 garlic clove, peeled and crushed
1–3 tsp curry paste, or to taste
225 g/8 oz basmati rice
400 g can aduki beans, drained and rinsed
225 ml/8 fl oz vegetable stock
125 g/4 oz firm tofu, crumbled
2 tbsp freshly chopped coriander
salt and freshly ground black pepper

FOR THE CARROT RAITA:
2 large carrots, peeled and grated
½ cucumber, cut into tiny dice
150 ml/¼ pint Greek yogurt

TO SERVE:
wholemeal baps
tomato slices
lettuce leaves

Heat 1 tablespoon of the oil in a saucepan and gently cook the onion for 10 minutes until soft. Add the garlic and curry paste and cook for a few more seconds. Stir in the rice and beans.

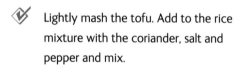

Pour in the stock, bring to the boil and simmer for 12 minutes, or until all the stock has been absorbed – do not lift the lid for the first 10 minutes of cooking. Reserve.

Lightly mash the tofu. Add to the rice mixture with the coriander, salt and pepper and mix.

Divide the mixture into four medium-sized or eight small burgers. Chill in the refrigerator for 30 minutes.

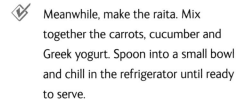
Meanwhile, make the raita. Mix together the carrots, cucumber and Greek yogurt. Spoon into a small bowl and chill in the refrigerator until ready to serve.

Heat the remaining oil in a large frying pan. Fry the burgers, in batches if necessary, for 4–5 minutes on each side, or until lightly browned. Serve in the baps with tomato slices and lettuce. Accompany with the raita.

Food Fact

Firm tofu is sold in blocks. It is made in a similar way to soft cheese and is the pressed curds of soya milk.

Mixed Grain Pilaf

Ingredients (Serves 4)

2 tbsp olive oil
1 garlic clove, peeled and crushed
¹/₂ tsp ground turmeric
125 g/4 oz mixed long-grain and wild rice
50 g/2 oz red lentils
300 ml/¹/₂ pint vegetable stock
200 g can chopped tomatoes
5 cm/2 inch piece cinnamon stick
salt and freshly ground black pepper
400 g can mixed beans, drained and rinsed

FOR THE OMELETTE:
15 g/¹/₂ oz margarine or butter
1 bunch spring onions, trimmed and finely sliced
3 medium eggs
4 tbsp freshly chopped herbs, such as parsley
 and chervil
fresh dill sprigs, to garnish

Heat 1 tablespoon of the oil in a saucepan. Add the garlic and turmeric and cook for a few seconds. Stir in the rice and lentils.

Add the stock, tomatoes and cinnamon. Season to taste with salt and pepper. Stir once and bring to the boil. Lower the heat, cover and simmer for 20 minutes until most of the stock is absorbed and the rice and lentils are tender.

Stir in the beans, replace the lid and leave to stand for 2–3 minutes to allow the beans to heat through.

While the rice is cooking, heat the remaining oil and margarine or butter in a frying pan. Add the spring onions and cook for 4–5 minutes until soft. Lightly beat the eggs with 2 tablespoons of the herbs, then season with salt and pepper.

Pour the egg mixture over the spring onions. Stir gently with a spatula over a low heat, drawing the mixture from the sides to the centre as the omelette sets. When almost set, stop stirring and cook for about 30 seconds until golden underneath.

Remove the omelette from the pan, roll up and slice into thin strips. Fluff the rice up with a fork and remove the cinnamon stick. Spoon onto serving plates, top with strips of omelette and the remaining chopped herbs. Garnish with sprigs of dill and serve.

Layered Cheese and Herb Potato Cake

Ingredients (Serves 4)

450 g/1 lb waxy potatoes
2 tbsp freshly snipped chives
1 tbsp freshly chopped parsley
125 g/4 oz mature Cheddar cheese
1 medium egg, beaten
1 tsp paprika
75 g/3 oz fresh white breadcrumbs
50 g/2 oz almonds, toasted and roughly chopped
salt and freshly ground black pepper
40 g/1 ½ oz margarine or butter, melted
mixed salad or steamed vegetables, to serve

Preheat the oven to 180°C/350°F/ Gas Mark 4. Lightly oil and line the base of a 18 cm/7 inch round cake tin with lightly oiled greaseproof paper or baking parchment. Peel and thinly slice the potatoes and reserve. Stir the chives, parsley, cheese and egg together in a small bowl and reserve. Mix the paprika into the breadcrumbs.

Sprinkle the almonds over the base of the lined tin. Cover with half the potatoes, arranging them in layers, then sprinkle with the paprika breadcrumb mixture and season to taste with salt and pepper.

Spoon the cheese and herb mixture over the breadcrumbs with a little more seasoning, then arrange the remaining potatoes on top. Drizzle over the melted margarine or butter and press the surface down firmly.

Bake in the preheated oven for 1¼ hours, or until golden and cooked through. Let the tin stand for 10 minutes before carefully turning out and serving in thick wedges. Serve immediately with salad or freshly cooked vegetables.

Helpful Hint
Check that the potatoes are tender all the way through by pushing a thin skewer through the centre. If the potatoes are still a little hard and the top is already brown enough, loosely cover with foil and continue cooking until done.

Creamy Vegetable Korma

Ingredients (Serves 4)

2 tbsp vegetable oil
1 large onion, peeled and chopped
2 garlic cloves, peeled and crushed
1–2 tbsp Korma curry powder or paste, or to taste
finely grated zest and juice of ½ lemon
50 g/2 oz ground almonds
400 ml/14 fl oz vegetable stock
450 g/1 lb potatoes, peeled and diced
450 g/1 lb mixed vegetables, such as cauliflower,
   carrots and turnip, cut into chunks
125 ml/4 fl oz single cream
3 tbsp freshly chopped coriander
salt and freshly ground black pepper
naan bread, to serve

Heat the oil in a large saucepan. Add the onion and cook for 5 minutes. Stir in the garlic and cook for a further 5 minutes, or until soft and just beginning to colour.

Stir in the curry powder or paste. Continue cooking over a low heat for 1 minute, stirring.

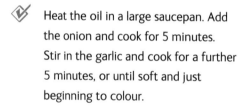

Stir in the lemon zest and juice and almonds. Blend in the vegetable stock. Slowly bring to the boil, stirring occasionally.

Add the potatoes and vegetables. Bring back to the boil, then reduce the heat, cover and simmer for 35–40 minutes until the vegetables are just tender. Check after 25 minutes and add a little more stock if needed.

Slowly stir in the cream and chopped coriander. Season to taste with salt and pepper. Cook very gently until heated through, but do not boil. Serve immediately with naan bread.

Chunky Vegetable and Fennel Goulash with Dumplings

Ingredients (Serves 4)

2 fennel bulbs, weighing about 450 g/1 lb
2 tbsp sunflower oil
1 large onion, peeled and sliced
1½ tbsp paprika
1 tbsp plain flour
300 ml/½ pint vegetable stock
400 g can whole peeled tomatoes, chopped
450 g/1 lb potatoes, peeled and cut into 2.5 cm/
    1 inch chunks
125 g/4 oz small button mushrooms
salt and freshly ground black pepper

FOR THE DUMPLINGS:
1 tbsp sunflower oil
1 small onion, peeled and finely chopped
1 medium egg
3 tbsp milk
3 tbsp freshly chopped parsley
125 g/4 oz fresh white breadcrumbs

 Cut the fennel in half widthways. Thickly slice the stalks and cut the bulbs into eight wedges. Heat the oil in a large saucepan or flameproof casserole dish. Add the onion and fennel and cook gently for 10 minutes until soft. Stir in the paprika and flour.

Remove from the heat and gradually stir in the stock. Add the chopped tomatoes, potatoes and mushrooms. Season to taste with salt and pepper. Bring to the boil, reduce the heat and simmer for 20 minutes.

Meanwhile, make the dumplings. Heat the oil in a frying pan and gently cook the onion for 10 minutes until soft. Leave to cool for a few minutes.

 In a bowl, beat the egg and milk together, then add the onion, parsley and breadcrumbs, and season to taste. With damp hands, form the mixture into 12 round dumplings each about the size of a walnut.

 Arrange the dumplings on top of the goulash. Cover and cook for a further 15 minutes, until the dumplings are cooked and the vegetables are tender. Serve immediately.

Tasty Tip
Soured cream or crème fraîche would be delicious spooned on top of the goulash.

Vegetarian Cassoulet

Ingredients (Serves 4)

225 g/8 oz dried haricot beans, soaked overnight
2 medium onions
1 bay leaf
1.5 litres/2 ½ pints cold water
550 g/1¼ lb large potatoes, peeled and cut into
   1 cm/½ inch slices
salt and freshly ground black pepper
5 tsp olive oil
1 large garlic clove, peeled and crushed
2 leeks, trimmed and sliced
200 g/7 oz canned whole peeled tomatoes, chopped
1 tsp dark muscovado sugar
1 tbsp freshly chopped thyme
2 tbsp freshly chopped parsley
3 courgettes, trimmed and sliced

FOR THE TOPPING:
50 g/2 oz fresh white breadcrumbs
25 g/1oz Cheddar cheese, finely grated

 Preheat the oven to 180°C/350°F/Gas Mark 4, 10 minutes before required. Drain the beans and rinse under cold running water, then place in a saucepan. Peel one of the onions and add to the beans with the bay leaf. Pour in the water. Bring to a rapid boil

and cook for 10 minutes, then turn down the heat, cover and simmer for 50 minutes, or until the beans are almost tender. Drain the beans, reserving the liquor, but discarding the onion and bay leaf.

 Cook the potatoes in a pan of lightly salted boiling water for 6–7 minutes until almost tender when tested with the point of a knife. Drain and reserve.

 Peel and chop the remaining onion. Heat the oil in a frying pan and cook the onion with the garlic and leeks for 10 minutes until softened. Stir in the tomatoes, sugar, thyme and parsley. Stir in the beans, with 300 ml/½ pint of the reserved liquor and season to taste. Simmer, uncovered, for 5 minutes.

 Layer the potato slices, courgettes and ladlefuls of the bean mixture in a large flameproof casserole dish. To make the topping, mix together the breadcrumbs and cheese and sprinkle over the top. Bake in the preheated oven for 40 minutes, or until the vegetables are cooked through and the topping is golden. Serve.

Leek and Potato Tart

Ingredients (Serves 4-6)

225 g/8 oz plain flour
pinch of salt
150 g/5 oz margarine or butter, cubed
50 g/2 oz walnuts, very finely chopped
1 large egg yolk

FOR THE FILLING:
450 g/1 lb leeks, trimmed and thinly sliced
40 g/1½ oz margarine or butter
450 g/1 lb large new potatoes, scrubbed
300 ml/½ pint soured cream
3 medium eggs, lightly beaten
125 g/4 oz Gruyère cheese, grated
freshly grated nutmeg
salt and freshly ground black pepper
fresh chives, to garnish

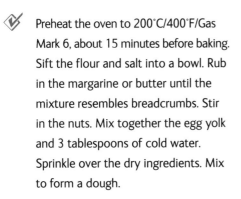

Preheat the oven to 200°C/400°F/Gas Mark 6, about 15 minutes before baking. Sift the flour and salt into a bowl. Rub in the margarine or butter until the mixture resembles breadcrumbs. Stir in the nuts. Mix together the egg yolk and 3 tablespoons of cold water. Sprinkle over the dry ingredients. Mix to form a dough.

Knead on a lightly floured surface for a few seconds, then wrap in clingfilm and chill in the refrigerator for 20 minutes. Roll out and use to line a 20 cm/8 inch springform tin or very deep flan tin. Chill for a further 30 minutes.

Cook the leeks in the margarine or butter over a high heat for 2–3 minutes, stirring constantly. Lower the heat, cover and cook for 10–15 minutes until soft, stirring occasionally. Remove the leeks from the heat.

Cook the potatoes in boiling salted water for 15 minutes, or until almost tender. Drain and thickly slice. Add to the leeks. Stir the soured cream into the leeks and potatoes, followed by the eggs, cheese, nutmeg and salt and pepper. Pour into the pastry case and bake on the middle shelf of the preheated oven for 20 minutes.

Reduce the oven temperature to 190°C/375°F/Gas Mark 5 and cook for a further 30–35 minutes until the filling is set. Garnish with chives and serve immediately.

Sicilian Baked Aubergine

Ingredients (Serves 4)

2 aubergines, trimmed
2 tbsp olive oil
2 celery stalks, trimmed
4 large ripe tomatoes
2 shallots, peeled and finely chopped
1½ tsp tomato purée
25 g/1 oz green pitted olives
25 g/1 oz black pitted olives
salt and freshly ground black pepper
1 tbsp white wine vinegar
2 tsp caster sugar
1 tbsp freshly chopped basil, to garnish
mixed salad leaves, to serve

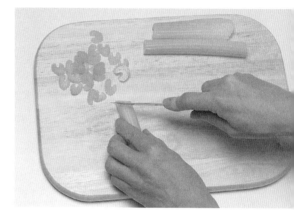

Preheat the oven to 200°C/400°F/Gas Mark 6. Cut the aubergines into small cubes and place on an oiled baking tray. Sprinkle with 1½ tablespoons of the oil.

Cover the tray with foil and bake in the preheated oven for 15–20 minutes until soft. Reserve, to allow the aubergine to cool.

Place the celery and tomatoes in a large bowl and cover with boiling water.

Remove the tomatoes from the bowl when their skins begin to peel away. Remove the skins, then deseed and chop the flesh into small pieces.

Remove the celery from the bowl of water, finely chop and reserve.

Pour the remaining oil into a nonstick saucepan, add the chopped shallots and fry gently for 2–3 minutes until soft. Add the celery, tomatoes, tomato purée and olives. Season to taste with salt and pepper.

Simmer gently for 3–4 minutes. Add the vinegar, sugar and cooled aubergine to the pan and heat gently for 2–3 minutes until all the ingredients are well blended. Reserve to allow the aubergine mixture to cool. When cool, garnish with the chopped basil and serve cold with salad leaves.

Food Fact

It has been suggested that foods that are purple in colour, such as aubergines, have particularly powerful antioxidants, which help the body to protect itself from disease and strengthen the organs.

Marinated Vegetable Kebabs

Ingredients (Serves 4)

2 small courgettes, cut into 2 cm/¾ inch pieces
½ green pepper, deseeded and cut into
   2.5 cm/1 inch pieces
½ red pepper, deseeded and cut into
   2.5 cm /1 inch pieces
½ yellow pepper, deseeded and cut into
   2.5 cm/1 inch pieces
8 baby onions, peeled
8 button mushrooms
8 cherry tomatoes
freshly chopped parsley, to garnish
freshly cooked couscous, to serve

FOR THE MARINADE:
1 tbsp light olive oil
4 tbsp white wine vinegar
2 tbsp light soy sauce
1 red chilli, deseeded and finely chopped
2 garlic cloves, peeled and crushed
2.5 cm/1 inch piece root ginger, peeled and
   finely grated

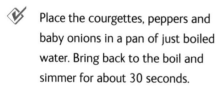

Place the courgettes, peppers and baby onions in a pan of just boiled water. Bring back to the boil and simmer for about 30 seconds.

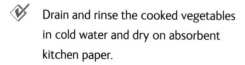

Drain and rinse the cooked vegetables in cold water and dry on absorbent kitchen paper.

Thread the cooked vegetables and the mushrooms and tomatoes alternately on to skewers and place in a large shallow dish.

Make the marinade by whisking all the ingredients together until thoroughly blended. Pour the marinade evenly over the kebabs, then chill in the refrigerator for at least 1 hour. Spoon the marinade over the kebabs occasionally during this time.

Place the kebabs in a hot griddle pan or on a hot barbecue and cook gently for 10–12 minutes. Turn the kebabs frequently and brush with the marinade when needed. When the vegetables are tender, sprinkle over the chopped parsley and serve immediately with couscous.

Tasty Tip

If using wooden skewers and cooking over a barbecue, soak the skewers in cold water for 30 minutes before using. Once the vegetables are threaded onto the skewers, wrap a small piece of kitchen foil around the ends of the skewers to prevent them burning.

Carrot and Parsnip Terrine

Ingredients (Serves 8-10)

550 g/1¼ lb carrots, peeled and chopped
450 g/1 lb parsnips, peeled and chopped
6 tbsp half-fat crème fraîche
450 g/1 lb spinach, rinsed
1 tbsp brown sugar
1 tbsp freshly chopped parsley
½ tsp freshly grated nutmeg
salt and freshly ground black pepper
6 medium eggs
fresh basil sprigs, to garnish

FOR THE TOMATO COULIS:
450 g/1 lb ripe tomatoes, deseeded and chopped
1 medium onion, peeled and finely chopped

Preheat the oven to 200°C/400°F/Gas Mark 6. Oil and line a 900 g/2 lb loaf tin with nonstick baking paper. Cook the carrots and parsnips in boiling salted water for 10–15 minutes or until very tender. Drain and purée separately. Add 2 tablespoons of the crème fraîche to both the carrots and the parsnips.

Steam the spinach for 5–10 minutes until very tender. Drain and squeeze out as much liquid as possible, then stir in the remaining crème fraîche.

Add the brown sugar to the carrot purée, the parsley to the parsnip mixture and the nutmeg to the spinach. Season all to taste with salt and pepper.

Beat 2 of the eggs, add to the spinach and turn into the tin. Add another 2 beaten eggs to the carrot mixture and layer carefully on top of the spinach. Beat the remaining eggs into the parsnip purée and layer on top of the terrine. Place the tin in a baking dish and pour in enough hot water to come halfway up the sides of the tin. Bake for 1 hour until a skewer inserted into the centre comes out clean. Leave to cool for at least 30 minutes. Run a sharp knife around the edges. Turn out on to a dish, garnish with basil sprigs and reserve.

Make the coulis by simmering the tomatoes and onions together for 5–10 minutes until slightly thickened. Season to taste. Blend well in a liquidiser and serve with the terrine.

Creamy Puy Lentils

Ingredients (Serves 4)

225 g/8 oz Puy lentils
1 tbsp olive oil
1 garlic clove, peeled and finely chopped
zest and juice of 1 lemon
1 tsp wholegrain mustard
1 tbsp freshly chopped tarragon
3 tbsp half-fat crème fraîche
salt and freshly ground black pepper
2 small tomatoes, deseeded and chopped
50 g/2 oz pitted black olives
1 tbsp freshly chopped parsley

TO GARNISH:
sprigs of fresh tarragon
lemon wedges

Put the lentils in a saucepan with plenty of cold water and bring to the boil.

Boil rapidly for 10 minutes, reduce the heat and simmer gently for a further 20 minutes until just tender. Drain well.

Meanwhile, prepare the dressing. Heat the oil in a frying pan over a medium heat.

Add the garlic and cook for about a minute until just beginning to brown. Add the lemon zest and juice.

Add the mustard and cook for a further 30 seconds.

Add the tarragon and crème fraîche and season to taste with salt and pepper.

Simmer and add the drained lentils, tomatoes and olives.

Transfer to a serving dish and sprinkle the chopped parsley on top.

Garnish the lentils with the tarragon sprigs and the lemon wedges and serve immediately.

Roasted Butternut Squash

Ingredients (Serves 4)

2 small butternut squash
4 garlic cloves, peeled and crushed
2 tbsp olive oil
salt and freshly ground black pepper
4 medium-sized leeks, trimmed, cleaned and
  thinly sliced
300 g can cannellini beans, drained and rinsed
125 g/4 oz fine French beans, halved
1 tbsp wholegrain mustard, or to taste
150 ml/¼ pint vegetable stock
50 g/2 oz rocket or watercress
2 tbsp freshly snipped chives
fresh chives, to garnish

TO SERVE:
4 tbsp low-fat fromage frais
mixed salad

Preheat the oven to 200°C/400°F/Gas Mark 6. Cut the butternut squash in half lengthways and scoop out all of the seeds.

Score the squash in a diamond pattern with a sharp knife. Mix the garlic with 1 tablespoon of the olive oil and brush over the cut surfaces of the squash. Season well with salt and pepper. Put on a baking sheet and roast for 40 minutes until tender.

Heat the remaining oil in a saucepan and fry the leeks for 5 minutes.

Add the drained cannellini beans, French beans, wholegrain mustard and vegetable stock. Bring to the boil and simmer gently for 5 minutes until the French beans are tender.

Remove from the heat and stir in the rocket or watercress and chives. Season well. Remove the squash from the oven and allow to cool for 5 minutes. Spoon in the bean mixture. Garnish with a few snipped chives and serve immediately with the fromage frais and a mixed salad.

Pumpkin and Chickpea Curry

Ingredients (Serves 4)

1 tbsp vegetable oil
1 small onion, peeled and sliced
2 garlic cloves, peeled and finely chopped
2.5 cm/1 inch piece root ginger, peeled and grated
1 tsp ground coriander
$\frac{1}{2}$ tsp ground cumin
$\frac{1}{2}$ tsp ground turmeric
$\frac{1}{4}$ tsp ground cinnamon
2 tomatoes, chopped
2 red bird's eye chillies, deseeded and finely chopped
450 g/1 lb pumpkin or butternut squash flesh, cubed
1 tbsp hot curry paste
300 ml/$\frac{1}{2}$ pint vegetable stock
1 large firm banana
400 g can chickpeas, drained and rinsed
salt and freshly ground black pepper
1 tbsp freshly chopped coriander
coriander sprigs, to garnish
rice or naan bread, to serve

Heat 1 tablespoon of the oil in a saucepan and add the onion. Fry gently for 5 minutes until softened.

Add the garlic, ginger and spices and fry for a further minute. Add the chopped tomatoes and chillies and cook for another minute.

Add the pumpkin and curry paste and fry gently for 3–4 minutes before adding the stock.

Stir well, bring to the boil and simmer for 20 minutes until the pumpkin is tender.

Thickly slice the banana and add to the pumpkin, along with the chickpeas. Simmer for a further 5 minutes.

Season to taste with salt and pepper and add the chopped coriander. Serve immediately, garnished with coriander sprigs and some rice or naan bread.

Helpful Hint

If preferred, use dried pulses, which will be less expensive than canned. To cook dried pulses, soak 125 g/4 oz of dried cannellini beans in plenty of water overnight. Drain and put into a saucepan with at least twice their volume of fresh water. Bring to the boil and boil rapidly for 10 minutes, then reduce the heat and simmer gently for a further 45–50 minutes until tender. Drain and use as above.

Tagliatelle with Broccoli

Ingredients (Serves 4)

450 g/1 lb broccoli, cut into florets
125 g/4 oz baby corn
350 g/12 oz dried tagliatelle
2 tbsp dark soy sauce
1 tbsp dark muscovado sugar
1–2 tbsp white wine vinegar
1 tbsp sunflower oil
2 garlic clove, peeled and finely chopped
2.5 cm/1 inch piece fresh root ginger, peeled and
  shredded
1 tsp dried chilli flakes, or to taste
radish slices, to garnish

Bring a large saucepan of salted water to the boil and add the broccoli and corn. Return the water to the boil then remove the vegetables at once using a slotted spoon, reserving the water. Plunge them into cold water and drain well. Dry on kitchen paper and reserve.

Return the water to the boil. Add the tagliatelle and cook until *al dente* or

according to the packet instructions. Drain well. Run under cold water until cold, then drain well again.

Place the soy sauce, sugar and vinegar into a bowl. Mix well, then reserve. Heat the oil in a wok or large frying pan over a high heat, add the garlic, ginger and chilli flakes and stir-fry for about 30 seconds. Add the broccoli and baby corn and continue to stir-fry for about 3 minutes.

Add the tagliatelle to the wok along with the soy sauce mixture and stir together for a further 1–2 minutes until heated through. Season to taste with salt and pepper. Garnish with the radish slices and serve immediately.

Baby Onion Risotto

Ingredients (Serves 4)

FOR THE BABY ONIONS:
1 tbsp olive oil
450 g/1 lb baby onions, peeled and halved if large
pinch sugar
1 tbsp freshly chopped thyme

FOR THE RISOTTO:
1 tbsp olive oil
1 small onion, peeled and finely chopped
2 garlic cloves, peeled and finely chopped
350 g/12 oz risotto rice
1.1 litres/2 pints hot vegetable stock
125 g/4 oz low-fat soft goats' cheese
salt and freshly ground black pepper
fresh thyme sprigs, to garnish
rocket leaves, to serve

 For the baby onions, heat the olive oil in a saucepan and add the onions with the sugar. Cover and cook over a low heat, stirring occasionally, for 20–25 minutes until caramelised. Uncover during the last 10 minutes of cooking.

 Meanwhile, for the risotto, heat the oil in a large frying pan and add the onion. Cook over a medium heat for 5 minutes until softened. Add the garlic and cook for a further 30 seconds.

 Add the risotto rice and stir well. Add the stock a ladleful at a time, stirring well and waiting until the last ladleful has been absorbed before stirring in the next. It will take 20–25 minutes to add all the stock, by which time the rice should be just cooked but still firm. Remove from the heat.

 Add the thyme to the onions and cook briefly. Increase the heat and allow the onion mixture to bubble for a few minutes. Add the onion mixture to the risotto along with the goats' cheese. Stir well and season to taste with salt and pepper. Garnish with fresh thyme sprigs. Serve immediately with the rocket leaves.

Spiced Couscous and Vegetables

Ingredients (Serves 4)

1 tbsp olive oil
1 large shallot, peeled and finely chopped
1 garlic clove, peeled and finely chopped
1 small red pepper, deseeded and cut into strips
1 small yellow pepper, deseeded and cut into strips
1 small aubergine, diced
1 tsp each turmeric, ground cumin, ground
    cinnamon and paprika
2 tsp ground coriander
large pinch saffron strands
2 tomatoes, peeled, deseeded and diced
2 tbsp lemon juice
225 g/8 oz couscous
225 ml/8 fl oz vegetable stock
2 tbsp raisins
2 tbsp whole almonds
2 tbsp freshly chopped parsley
2 tbsp freshly chopped coriander
salt and freshly ground black pepper

Heat the oil in a large frying pan, add the shallot and garlic and cook for 2–3 minutes until softened. Add the peppers and aubergine and reduce the heat.

Cook for 8–10 minutes until the vegetables are tender, adding a little water if necessary.

Test a piece of aubergine to ensure it is cooked through. Add all the spices and cook for a further minute, stirring.

Increase the heat and add the tomatoes and lemon juice. Cook for 2–3 minutes until the tomatoes have started to break down. Remove from the heat and leave to cool slightly.

Meanwhile, put the couscous into a large bowl. Bring the stock to the boil in a saucepan, then pour over the couscous. Stir well and cover with a clean tea towel.

Leave to stand for 7–8 minutes until all the stock is absorbed and the couscous has plumped up.

Uncover the couscous and fluff with a fork. Stir in the vegetable and spice mixture along with the raisins, almonds, parsley and coriander. Season to taste with salt and pepper and serve.

Black Bean Chilli with Avocado Salsa

Ingredients (Serves 4)

250 g/9 oz black beans or black-eye beans,
   soaked overnight
2 tbsp olive oil
1 large onion, peeled and finely chopped
1 red pepper, deseeded and diced
2 garlic cloves, peeled and finely chopped
1 red chilli, deseeded and finely chopped
2 tsp chilli powder
1 tsp ground cumin
2 tsp ground coriander
400 g can whole peeled tomatoes, chopped
450 ml/$^3/_4$ pint vegetable stock
1 small ripe avocado, diced
$^1/_2$ small red onion, peeled and finely chopped
2 tbsp freshly chopped coriander
juice of 1 lime
1 small tomato, peeled, deseeded and diced
salt and freshly ground black pepper
25 g/1 oz dark chocolate

TO GARNISH:
half-fat crème fraîche
lime slices
coriander sprigs

Drain the beans and place in a large saucepan with at least twice their volume of fresh water.

Bring slowly to the boil, skimming off any froth that rises to the surface. Boil rapidly for 10 minutes, then reduce the heat and simmer for about 45 minutes, adding more water if necessary. Drain and reserve.

Heat the oil in a large saucepan and add the onion and pepper. Cook for 3–4 minutes until softened. Add the garlic and chilli. Cook for 5 minutes, or until the onion and pepper have softened. Add the chilli powder, cumin and coriander and cook for 30 seconds. Add the beans along with the tomatoes and stock.

Bring to the boil and simmer uncovered for 40–45 minutes until the beans and vegetables are tender and the sauce has reduced.

Mix together the avocado, onion, fresh coriander, lime juice and tomato. Season with salt and pepper and set aside. Remove the chilli from the heat.

Break the chocolate into pieces. Sprinkle over the chilli. Leave for 2 minutes. Stir well. Garnish with crème fraîche, lime and coriander. Serve with the avocado salsa.

Recipes: Baking & Desserts

Bacon and Tomato Breakfast Twist

Ingredients (Serves 4)

450 g/1 lb strong white flour
$^1/_2$ tsp salt
7 g sachet easy-blend dried yeast
300 ml/$^1/_2$ pint warm milk
15 g/$^1/_2$ oz margarine or butter, melted

FOR THE FILLING:
225 g/8 oz back bacon, rind removed
15 g/$^1/_2$ oz margarine or butter, melted
175 g/6 oz ripe tomatoes, peeled,
   deseeded and chopped
freshly ground black pepper

TO FINISH:
beaten egg, to glaze
2 tsp medium oatmeal

✓ Preheat the oven to 200°C/400°F/Gas Mark 6, 15 minutes before baking. Sift the flour and salt into a large bowl. Stir in the yeast and make a well in the centre. Pour in the milk and margarine or butter and mix to a soft dough.

✓ Knead on a lightly floured surface for 10 minutes, until smooth and elastic. Put in an oiled bowl, cover with clingfilm and leave to rise in a warm place for 1 hour, until doubled in size.

✓ Cook the bacon under a hot grill for 5–6 minutes, turning once, until crisp. Leave to cool, then roughly chop.

✓ Knead the dough again for a minute or two. Roll it out to a 25 x 33 cm/ 10 x 13 inch rectangle. Cut in half lengthways. Lightly brush with margarine or butter, then scatter with the bacon, tomatoes and black pepper, leaving a 1 cm/$^1/_2$ inch margin around the edges. Brush the edges of the dough with beaten egg, then roll up each rectangle lengthways.

✓ Place the 2 rolls side by side and twist together, pinching the ends to seal. Transfer to an oiled baking sheet and loosely cover with oiled clingfilm. Leave to rise in a warm place for 30 minutes. Brush with the beaten egg and sprinkle with the oatmeal. Bake in the preheated oven for about 30 minutes, or until golden brown and hollow-sounding when tapped on the base. Serve the bread warm in thick slices.

Spicy Filled Naan Bread

Ingredients (Makes 6)

400 g/14 oz strong white flour
1 tsp salt
1 tsp easy-blend dried yeast
15 g/½ oz margarine or butter, melted
1 tsp clear honey
200 ml/7 fl oz warm water

FOR THE FILLING:
25 g/1 oz margarine or butter, melted
1 small onion, peeled and finely chopped
1 garlic clove, peeled and crushed
1 tsp ground coriander
1 tsp ground cumin
2 tsp grated fresh root ginger
pinch of chilli powder
pinch of ground cinnamon
salt and freshly ground black pepper

Preheat the oven to 220°C/450°F/Gas Mark 8, 15 minutes before baking. Place a large baking sheet in to heat up. Sift the flour and salt into a large bowl. Stir in the yeast and make a well in the centre. Add the margarine or butter, the honey and the warm water. Mix to a soft dough.

Knead the dough on a lightly floured surface, until smooth and elastic. Put in a lightly oiled bowl, cover with clingfilm and leave to rise for 1 hour, or until doubled in size.

For the filling, melt the margarine or butter in a frying pan and gently cook the onion for about 5 minutes. Stir in the garlic and spices and season to taste with salt and pepper. Cook for a further 6–7 minutes until soft. Remove from the heat, stir in 1 tablespoon water and leave to cool.

Briefly knead the dough, then divide into six pieces. Roll out each piece of dough to a 12 cm/ 5 inch round. Spoon the filling on to one half of each round.

Fold over and press the edges together to seal. Re-roll to shape into flat ovals, about 16 cm/6 inches long.

Cover with oiled clingfilm and leave to rise for about 15 minutes.

Transfer the breads to the hot baking sheet and cook in the preheated oven for 10–12 minutes, until puffed up and lightly browned. Serve hot.

Quick Brown Bread

Ingredients
(Makes 2 x 450g/1 lb loaves)

700 g/1½ lb strong wholemeal flour
2 tsp salt
½ tsp caster sugar
7 g sachet easy-blend dried yeast
450 ml/¾ pint warm water

TO FINISH:
beaten egg, to glaze
1 tbsp plain white flour, to dust

Preheat the oven to 200°C/400°F/Gas Mark 6, 15 minutes before baking. Oil two 450 g/1 lb loaf tins. Sift the flour, salt and sugar into a large bowl, adding the remaining bran in the sieve. Stir in the yeast, then make a well in the centre.

Pour the warm water into the dry ingredients and mix to form a soft dough, adding a little more water if needed.

Knead on a lightly floured surface for 10 minutes, until smooth and elastic.

Divide in half, shape into 2 oblongs and place in the tins. Cover with oiled clingfilm and leave in a warm place for 40 minutes, or until risen to the top of the tins.

Glaze one loaf with the beaten egg and dust the other loaf generously with the plain flour.

Bake the loaves in the preheated oven for 35 minutes or until well risen and lightly browned. Turn out of the tins and return to the oven for 5 minutes to crisp the sides. Cool on a wire rack.

Helpful Hint
For most breads the dough is kneaded, left to rise, kneaded, shaped and then left to rise again. This bread does not need the first rising.

Maple, Pecan and Lemon Loaf

Ingredients
(Cuts into 12 slices)

350 g/12 oz plain flour
1 tsp baking powder
175 g/6 oz margarine or butter, cubed
75 g/3 oz caster sugar
125 g/4 oz pecan nuts, roughly chopped
3 medium eggs
1 tbsp milk
finely grated zest of 1 lemon
5 tbsp maple syrup

FOR THE ICING:
75 g/3 oz icing sugar
1 tbsp lemon juice
25 g/1 oz pecans, roughly chopped

Preheat the oven to 170°C/325°F/Gas Mark 3, 10 minutes before baking. Lightly oil and line the base of a 900 g/2 lb loaf tin with nonstick baking parchment.

Sift the flour and baking powder into a large bowl.

Rub in the margarine or butter until the mixture resembles fine breadcrumbs. Stir in the caster sugar and pecan nuts.

Beat the eggs together with the milk and lemon zest. Stir in the maple syrup. Add to the dry ingredients and gently stir in until mixed thoroughly to make a soft dropping consistency.

Spoon the mixture into the prepared tin and level the top with the back of a spoon. Bake on the middle shelf of the preheated oven for 50–60 minutes until the cake is well risen and lightly browned. If a skewer inserted into the centre comes out clean, then the cake is ready.

Leave the cake in the tin for about 10 minutes, then turn out and leave to cool on a wire rack. Carefully remove the lining paper.

Sift the icing sugar into a small bowl and stir in the lemon juice to make a smooth icing.

Drizzle the icing over the top of the loaf, then scatter with the chopped pecans. Leave to set, thickly slice and serve.

Iced Bakewell Tart

Ingredients (Cuts into 8 slices)

FOR THE PASTRY:
175 g/6 oz plain flour
pinch salt
60 g/2 ½ oz margarine or butter,
   cut into small pieces
50 g/2 oz white vegetable fat,
   cut into small pieces
2 small egg yolks, beaten

FOR THE FILLING:
125 g/4 oz margarine or butter, melted
125 g/4 oz caster sugar
125 g/4 oz ground almonds
2 large eggs, beaten
few drops almond essence
2 tbsp seedless raspberry jam

FOR THE ICING:
125 g/4 oz icing sugar, sifted
6–8 tsp fresh lemon juice
25 g/1 oz toasted flaked almonds

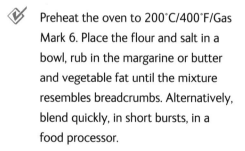

Preheat the oven to 200°C/400°F/Gas Mark 6. Place the flour and salt in a bowl, rub in the margarine or butter and vegetable fat until the mixture resembles breadcrumbs. Alternatively, blend quickly, in short bursts, in a food processor.

Add the eggs, with sufficient water to make a soft, pliable dough. Knead lightly on a floured board then chill in the refrigerator for about 30 minutes. Roll out the pastry and use to line a 23 cm/9 inch loose-bottomed flan tin.

For the filling, mix together the melted margarine or butter, sugar, almonds and beaten eggs and add a few drops of almond essence. Spread the base of the pastry case with the raspberry jam and spoon over the egg mixture.

Bake in the preheated oven for about 30 minutes until the filling is firm and golden brown. Remove from the oven and allow to cool completely.

When the tart is cold, make the icing by mixing together the icing sugar and lemon juice, a little at a time, until the icing is smooth and of a spreadable consistency.

Spread the icing over the tart, leave to set for 2–3 minutes and sprinkle with the almonds. Chill in the refrigerator for about 10 minutes and serve.

Chocolate and Fruit Crumble

Ingredients (Serves 4)

FOR THE CRUMBLE:
125 g/4 oz plain flour
125 g/4 oz margarine or butter
75 g/3 oz light soft brown sugar
50 g/2 oz rolled porridge oats
50 g/2 oz hazelnuts, chopped

FOR THE FILLING:
450 g/1 lb Bramley apples
1 tbsp lemon juice
50 g/2 oz sultanas
50 g/2 oz seedless raisins
50 g/2 oz light soft brown sugar
350 g/12 oz pears, peeled, cored and chopped
1 tsp ground cinnamon
125 g/4 oz plain dark chocolate, very roughly chopped
2 tsp caster sugar for sprinkling

 Preheat the oven to 190°C/375°F/Gas Mark 5, 10 minutes before baking. Lightly oil an ovenproof dish.

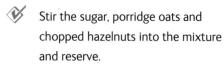 For the crumble, sift the flour into a large bowl. Cut the margarine or butter into small dice and add to the flour. Rub the margarine or butter into the flour until the mixture resembles fine breadcrumbs.

Stir the sugar, porridge oats and chopped hazelnuts into the mixture and reserve.

For the filling, peel the apples, core and slice thickly. Place in a large heavy-based saucepan with the lemon juice and 3 tablespoons water. Add the sultanas, raisins and soft brown sugar.

Bring slowly to the boil, cover and simmer over a gentle heat for 8–10 minutes, stirring occasionally, until the apples are slightly softened.

Remove the saucepan from the heat and leave to cool slightly before stirring in the pears, ground cinnamon and the chopped chocolate.

Spoon into the prepared ovenproof dish. Sprinkle the crumble evenly over the top then bake in the preheated oven for 35–40 minutes until the top is golden. Remove from the oven, sprinkle with the caster sugar and serve immediately.

Tasty Tip
Bramley apples have a sharp flavour and may need more sugar than other apples. Their advantage is that they are ideal for cooking and will form a purée very easily. If you prefer, use a dessert apple such as Golden Delicious or Granny Smith.

Fruity Roulade

Ingredients (Serves 4)

FOR THE SPONGE:
3 medium eggs
75 g/3 oz caster sugar
75 g/3 oz plain flour, sifted
1–2 tbsp caster sugar for sprinkling

FOR THE FILLING:
125 g/4 oz Quark
125 g/4 oz half-fat Greek yogurt
25 g/1 oz caster sugar
1 tbsp orange liqueur (optional)
grated zest of 1 orange
125 g/4 oz strawberries, hulled and cut into quarters

TO DECORATE:
strawberries
sifted icing sugar

Preheat the oven to 220°C/425°F/Gas Mark 7. Lightly oil and line a 33 x 23 cm/13 x 9 inch Swiss roll tin with greaseproof paper or baking parchment.

Using an electric whisk, whisk the eggs and sugar until the mixture is double in volume and leaves a trail across the top.

Fold in the flour with a metal spoon or rubber spatula. Pour into the prepared tin and bake in the preheated oven for 10–12 minutes until well risen and golden.

Place a whole sheet of greaseproof paper or baking parchment out on a flat work surface and sprinkle evenly with caster sugar.

Turn the cooked sponge out on to the paper, discard the paper, trim the sponge and roll up encasing the paper inside. Reserve until cool.

To make the filling, mix together the Quark, yogurt, caster sugar, liqueur (if using) and orange zest. Unroll the roulade and spread over the mixture. Scatter over the strawberries and roll up.

Decorate the roulade with the strawberries. Dust with the icing sugar and serve.

Oaty Fruit Puddings

Ingredients (Serves 4)

125 g/4 oz rolled oats
50 g/2 oz low-fat spread, melted
2 tbsp chopped almonds
1 tbsp clear honey
pinch ground cinnamon
2 pears, peeled, cored and finely chopped
1 tbsp marmalade
orange zest, to decorate
low-fat custard or fruit-flavoured low-fat yogurt,
    to serve

Preheat the oven to 200°C/400°F/Gas Mark 6. Lightly oil and line the bases of four individual pudding bowls or muffin tins with small circles of greaseproof paper.

Mix together the oats, low-fat spread, nuts, honey and cinnamon in a small bowl.

Using a spoon, spread two thirds of the oaty mixture over the base and the sides of the pudding bowls or muffin tins.

Toss together the pears and marmalade and spoon into the oaty cases.

Scatter over the remaining oaty mixture to cover the pears and marmalade.

Bake in the preheated oven for 15–20 minutes until cooked and the tops of the puddings are golden and crisp.

Leave for 5 minutes before removing the pudding bowls or the muffin tins. Decorate with orange zest and serve hot with low-fat custard or low-fat fruit-flavoured yogurt.

Helpful Hint
Seasonal fruit and vegetables are cheaper than fruit that have been shipped over many miles. Most fruit works well in this recipe, from apples and pears to gooseberries and currants.

Lemon Surprise

Ingredients (Serves 4)

75 g/3 oz margarine or butter
175 g/6 oz caster sugar
3 medium eggs, separated
75 g/3 oz self-raising flour
450 ml/¾ pint semi-skimmed milk
juice of 2 lemons
juice of 1 orange
2 tsp icing sugar
lemon twists, to decorate (optional)
sliced strawberries, to serve (optional)

Preheat the oven to 190°C/375°F/Gas Mark 5. Lightly oil a deep ovenproof dish.

Beat together the margarine or butter and sugar until pale and fluffy.

Add the egg yolks, one at a time, with 1 tablespoon of the flour. Beat well after each addition. Once added, stir in the remaining flour.

Stir in the milk, 4 tablespoons of the lemon juice and 3 tablespoons of the orange juice.

Whisk the egg whites until stiff and fold into the pudding mixture with a metal spoon or rubber spatula until well combined. Pour into the prepared dish.

Stand the dish in a roasting tin and pour in just enough boiling water to come halfway up the sides of the dish.

 Remove the pudding from the oven and sprinkle with the icing sugar. If liked, decorate with the lemon twists and serve immediately with the strawberries.

Food Fact

This recipe uses a *bain-marie* – when the dish is placed in a tin half-filled with hot water to enable the pudding to cook slowly.

 Bake in the preheated oven for 45 minutes until well risen and spongy to the touch.

Raspberry Sorbet Crush

Ingredients (Serves 4)

225 g/8 oz raspberries, thawed if frozen
grated zest and juice of 1 lime
300 ml/¹/₂ pint orange juice
225 g/8 oz caster sugar
2 medium egg whites

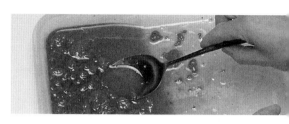

Set the freezer to rapid freeze. If using fresh raspberries, pick over and lightly rinse.

Place the raspberries in a dish and, using a masher, mash to a chunky purée.

Place the lime zest and juice, orange juice and half the caster sugar in a large heavy-based saucepan.

Heat gently, stirring frequently, until the sugar is dissolved. Bring to the boil and boil rapidly for about 5 minutes.

Remove the pan from the heat and pour carefully into a freezable container.

Leave to cool, then place in the freezer and freeze for 2 hours, stirring occasionally to break up the ice crystals.

Fold the ice mixture into the raspberry purée with a metal spoon and freeze for a further 2 hours, stirring occasionally.

Whisk the egg whites until stiff. Then gradually whisk in the remaining caster sugar a tablespoon at a time until the egg white mixture is stiff and glossy.

Fold into the raspberry sorbet with a metal spoon and freeze for 1 hour. Spoon into tall glasses and serve immediately. Remember to return the freezer to its normal setting.

Food Fact
This recipe contains raw egg and should not be given to babies, young children, pregnant women, the sick, the elderly and those suffering from a recurring illness.

Carrot Cake

Ingredients (Cuts into 8 slices)

200 g/7 oz plain flour
½ tsp ground cinnamon
½ tsp freshly grated nutmeg
1 tsp baking powder
1 tsp bicarbonate of soda
150 g/5 oz dark muscovado sugar
200 ml/7 fl oz vegetable oil
3 medium eggs
225 g/8 oz carrots, peeled and roughly grated
50 g/2 oz chopped walnuts

FOR THE ICING:
175 g/6 oz cream cheese
finely grated zest of 1 orange
1 tbsp orange juice
1 tsp vanilla essence
125 g/4 oz icing sugar

Preheat the oven to 150°C/300°F/Gas Mark 2, 10 minutes before baking. Lightly oil and line the base of a 15 cm/ 6 inch deep square cake tin with greaseproof paper or baking parchment.

Sift the flour, spices, baking powder and bicarbonate of soda together into a large bowl.

Stir in the dark muscovado sugar and mix together.

Lightly whisk the oil and eggs together, then gradually stir into the flour and sugar mixture. Stir well.

Add the carrots and walnuts. Mix thoroughly, then pour into the prepared cake tin. Bake in the preheated oven for 1¼ hours, or until light and springy to the touch and a skewer inserted into the centre of the cake comes out clean.

Remove from the oven and allow to cool in the tin for 5 minutes, then turn out on to a wire rack. Leave until cold.

To make the icing, beat together the cream cheese, orange zest, orange juice and vanilla essence. Sift the icing sugar and stir into the cream cheese mixture.

When cold, discard the lining paper, spread the cream cheese icing over the top and serve cut into squares.

Gingerbread

Ingredients (Cuts into 8 slices)

175 g/6 oz margarine or butter
225 g/8 oz black treacle
50 g/2 oz dark muscovado sugar
350 g/12 oz plain flour
2 tsp ground ginger
150 ml/¼ pint milk, warmed
2 medium eggs
1 tsp bicarbonate of soda
1 piece of stem ginger in syrup
1 tbsp stem ginger syrup

Preheat the oven to 150°C/300°C/ Gas Mark 2, 10 minutes before baking. Lightly oil and line the base of a 20 cm/8 inch deep round cake tin with greaseproof paper or baking parchment.

In a saucepan gently heat the butter or margarine, black treacle and sugar, stirring occasionally until the butter melts. Leave to cool slightly.

Sift the flour and ground ginger into a large bowl.

Make a well in the centre, then pour in the treacle mixture. Reserve 1 tablespoon of the milk, then pour the rest into the treacle mixture. Stir together lightly until mixed.

Beat the eggs together, then stir into the mixture.

Dissolve the bicarbonate of soda in the remaining 1 tablespoon of warmed milk and add to the mixture.

Beat the mixture until well mixed and free of lumps.

Pour into the prepared tin and bake in the preheated oven for 1 hour, or until well risen and a skewer inserted into the centre comes out clean.

 Cool in the tin, then remove. Slice the stem ginger into thin slivers and sprinkle over the cake. Drizzle with the syrup and serve.

Food Fact

There are many different types of gingerbread, ranging in colour from a deep rich dark brown to a light golden. This is due to the type of treacle and the amount of bicarbonate of soda used. One well-known gingerbread from Yorkshire is parkin, which uses both golden syrup and black treacle.

Index